HEZEKIAH

CHARACTERS OF THE BIBLE SERIES
BY JIMMY SWAGGART:

Abraham

David

Elijah

Elisha

Great Women of the Bible, Old Testament

Great Women of the Bible, New Testament

Hezekiah

Jacob

Joseph

Noah

Paul, The Apostle

HEZEKIAH

JIMMY SWAGGART

JIMMY SWAGGART MINISTRIES
P.O. Box 262550 | Baton Rouge, Louisiana 70826-2550
www.jsm.org

ISBN 978-1-941403-36-5

09-146 | COPYRIGHT © 2017 Jimmy Swaggart Ministries®

17 18 19 20 21 22 23 24 25 26 / EBM / 10 9 8 7 6 5 4 3 2 1

TABLE OF CONTENTS

HEZEKIAH

INTRODUCTION

INTRODUCTION

A little bit short of a thousand years before Christ, the nation of Israel broke apart, one might say. The two tribes of Judah and Benjamin remained with the southern kingdom called Judah. The balance of the tribes, referred to as the northern kingdom, went under the name of Israel or Samaria. Rehoboam, Solomon's son, became king of the southern confederation, with Jeroboam becoming king of the northern confederation.

About 250 years from that particular time, Hezekiah began to reign over the southern kingdom of Judah. He was one of the godliest kings who graced that particular throne, which, incidentally, was the most important throne on the face of the earth. It was that because Judah then was the only nation in the world that had any semblance of the knowledge of God. This means that Judah was monotheistic in that she believed in one God—Jehovah. Every other nation in the world was polytheistic, meaning they worshipped many gods, actually demon spirits. This is the reason that Judah was so very, very important in the eyes of God, and for the benefit of the balance of the world, even though other nations would not have known this.

HEZEKIAH

Strangely enough, Hezekiah was the son of one of the most wicked kings of Judah—Ahaz. As well, possibly one could say that the most wicked king to grace the throne of Judah was Hezekiah's son, Manasseh. Concerning Hezekiah, the Holy Spirit says of him, *"And he did that which was right in the sight of the Lord, according to all that David his father had done"* (II Chron. 29:2).

David was always used as the yardstick or example. That which is *right in the sight of God* is all that matters; unfortunately, the church all too often cares little about what is right in God's eyes, making their own eyes the yardstick. Because of Hezekiah's consecration to the Lord, he was blessed abundantly, which means that Judah was abundantly blessed.

THE PROPHET ISAIAH

During the reign of Hezekiah, most of the ministry of the Prophet Isaiah served as a great strength for the nation of Judah. As well, Hezekiah greatly leaned on the consecration of this godly man. Isaiah is referred to as the millennial prophet, meaning that he said more about the coming kingdom age than any other prophet. His great predictions are yet to be fulfilled but most definitely shall be.

When Hezekiah died, the Scripture says, *"And Hezekiah slept with his fathers, and they buried him in the chiefest of the sepulchres of the sons of David: and all Judah and the inhabitants of Jerusalem did him honor at his death"* (II Chron. 32:33).

Lord, I care not for riches,
Neither silver nor gold,
I would make sure of heaven,
I would enter the fold.
In the book of Your kingdom,
With its pages so fair,
Tell me, Jesus, my Saviour,
Is my name written there?

Lord, my sins they are many,
Like the sands of the sea,
But Your blood, O my Saviour,
Is sufficient for me;
For Your promise is written,
In bright letters that glow,
"Though your sins be as scarlet,
I will make them like snow."

Oh! That beautiful city,
With its mansions of light,
With its glorified beings,
In pure garments of white;
Where no evil thing comes
To despoil what is fair;
Where the angels are watching,
Yes, my name's written there.

HEZEKIAH

CHAPTER 1

HEZEKIAH AND DAVID

HEZEKIAH AND DAVID

"Hezekiah began to reign when he was five and twenty years old, and he reigned nine and twenty years in Jerusalem. And his mother's name was Abijah, the daughter of Zechariah. And he did that which was right in the sight of the Lord, according to all that David his father had done" (II Chron. 29:1-2).

THAT WHICH IS RIGHT

David was always used as the yardstick or example.

That which is *right in the sight of God* is all that matters. Unfortunately, the church all too often cares little about what is right in God's eyes, making their own eyes the yardstick. Thankfully, now would begin a time of revival for Judah.

The Scripture says that Ahaz was 20 years old when he began to reign and that he reigned 16 years, which means that he was 36 years old when he died.

The Scripture also says that Hezekiah was 25 years old when he began to reign. Some have concluded from that that Ahaz was only 11 years old when Hezekiah was born. That is not the case!

Even though the Scripture doesn't say, more than likely, Hezekiah was born when Ahaz was about 20 years old, or perhaps a little younger. Once again, even though the Scripture doesn't say one way or the other, more than likely, it could have been several years after Ahaz died before Hezekiah actually took the throne, which is probably what happened.

IN THE SIGHT OF THE LORD

The Scripture says that Ahaz, Hezekiah's father *"did not that which was right in the sight of the Lord, like David his father* (his father quite a few times removed)*"* (II Chron. 28:1). Then he said concerning Hezekiah, *"And he did that which was right in the sight of the Lord, according to all that David his father had done."* How refreshing!

As we said previously, David was always used as the example. Why?

Two reasons:

1. First and foremost, David was chosen by God to be the man through whose lineage the Son of God, the son of David, would be born. That's the reason that the Gospel according to Matthew begins with the words, *"The book of the generation of Jesus Christ, the Son of David, the Son of Abraham"* (Mat. 1:1). Abraham was the titular leader of the family of Israel, having been chosen by God for that purpose (Gen. 12:1-3). So, the nation of Israel came from the loins of Abraham

and the womb of Sarah. However, it was David in the nation of Israel who was chosen by the Lord to be in the lineage of Christ, the greatest honor that could ever be paid a human being. So, at the time of Christ, our Lord was often referred to as the *"Son of David"* (Mk. 10:47). Admittedly, the religious leaders of Israel did not refer to the Master in that capacity, but others did, such as Bartimaeus, proving that it was known that the Messiah would be the *"Son of David."* Tragically, the religious leadership of Israel did not recognize our Lord as their Messiah! They have suffered immeasurably for that decision.

NO PERFECT PEOPLE BUT A PERFECT CHRIST

2. Even though David failed at times, and failed miserably, the second reason that he was chosen by the Lord to be in the lineage of the Messiah is because he was always quick to repent and to take the blame personally for what had been done, whatever it was. Unfortunately, there are no perfect people, but fortunately, there is a perfect Christ.

As well, when the Lord forgives someone, that person is totally and completely forgiven. That means that no matter how dastardly the sin committed was, in the mind of God, that sin no longer exists and is completely taken away. It's called *"justification by faith."*

When David committed the horrible sin of adultery with Bath-sheba, and even worse than that, murdered her husband in cold blood, he could not go to the Law for mercy because there is no mercy in law. So, he had to reach back to the deliverance of the children of Israel from Egyptian bondage when the blood was applied to the doorposts of the homes (such as they were) of the Israelites in Egypt, meaning they were spared.

God had said:

"And the blood shall be to you for a token upon the houses where you are (the blood applied to the doorposts meant that their faith and trust were in the paschal lamb; the blood then applied was only a 'token,' meaning that it was then but a symbol of One who was to come, who would redeem mankind by the shedding of His life's blood)."

WHEN I SEE THE BLOOD

The entire phrase is:

And the blood shall be to you for a token upon the houses where you are: and when I see the blood, I will pass over you (this is, without a doubt, one of the single most important Scriptures in the entirety of the Word of God; the lamb had taken the fatal blow, and because it had taken the blow, those in the house would be spared; it was not a question of personal worthiness, self had nothing whatever to do in the matter; it was a matter of faith; all under the cover of the blood were safe, just as all presently under the cover of the blood are safe; this means that they were not merely in a savable state, but rather that they were 'saved'; as well, they were not partly saved and partly exposed to judgment; they were wholly saved because there is no such thing as partial justification; the Lord didn't say, 'When I see you,' or 'When I see your good works,' etc., but, 'When I see the blood'; this speaks of Christ and what He would do at the Cross in order that we might be saved, which pertained to Him giving Himself in sacrifice, which necessitated the shedding of His precious blood [I Pet. 1:18-19]), *and the plague shall not be upon you to destroy you, when I smite the land of Egypt.* (Salvation from the 'plague' of judgment is afforded only by the shed blood of the Lamb, and faith in that shed blood) (Ex. 12:13) (The Expositor's Study Bible).

DAVID'S PRAYER OF REPENTANCE

In David's prayer of repentance (and I continue to quote from The Expositor's Study Bible) he said the following:

"Have mercy upon me, O God, according to Your lovingkindness: according unto the multitude of Your tender mercies blot out my transgressions. (This is a psalm of David, written when Nathan the prophet came unto him after the sin with Bath-sheba and the murder of her husband Uriah [II Sam., Chpt. 12]."

George Williams said:

"This psalm was given by the Holy Spirit to David when, his heart broken and contrite because of his sin against God, he pleaded for pardon through the atoning blood of the Lamb of God, foreshadowed in Exodus, Chapter 12. Thus, he was not only fittingly provided with a vehicle of expression in repentance and faith, but he was also used as a channel of prophetic communication.'

ISRAEL

George Williams continues:

"David, in his sin, repentance, and restoration is a forepicture of Israel. For as he forsook the Law and was guilty of adultery and murder, so Israel despised the covenant, turned aside to idolatry [spiritual adultery], and murdered the Messiah. Thus the scope and structure of this psalm goes far beyond David. It predicts the future confession and forgiveness of Israel in the day of the Messiah's second coming, when, looking upon Him whom they pierced, they shall mourn and weep [Zech., Chpts. 12-13].'

THE INTERCESSORY WORK OF CHRIST

"As well, this prayer is even more perfectly a vivid portrayal of the intercessory work of Christ on behalf of His people. Even though David prayed this prayer, the Son of David would make David's sin [as well as ours] His own, and pray through Him that which must be said. This means that this is the truest prayer of repentance ever prayed because it symbolizes the intercessory work of the Son of David.)

"Wash me thoroughly from my iniquity, and cleanse me from my sin (man's problem is sin, and man must admit that; the only remedy for sin, and I mean the only remedy, is 'Jesus Christ and Him crucified,' to which David, in essence, appealed [Heb. 10:12]; the blood of Jesus Christ alone cleanses from all sin [I Jn. 1:7])

THE ACKNOWLEDGMENT OF SIN

"For I acknowledge my transgressions: and my sin is ever before me (the acknowledgment of verses 3 and 4 is the condition of divine forgiveness; all sin, in essence, is committed against God; therefore, God demands that the transgressions be acknowledged, placing the blame where it rightfully belongs—on the perpetrator; He cannot and, in fact, will not forgive sin that is not acknowledged and for which no responsibility is taken)" (Ps. 51:1-3) (The Expositor's Study Bible).

There is a teaching that is making advancement today that states that a believer does not have to confess sin, does not have to admit sin, and if, in fact, sin is present, it is to be ignored. The idea is that Jesus makes intercession for us, so there is nothing required on our part.

As we have just stated, nothing could be more wrong than that. We must acknowledge our sin, and the only way to properly do that is to confess it before the Lord.

John wrote that if we confess our sins, He is faithful to forgive us of all sin, and to cleanse us from all unrighteousness (I Jn. 1:9).

Our detractors claim that this is for the unredeemed and not for believers. In the first place, such is ridiculous. It is impossible for unbelievers to confess all of their sins. While the unredeemed can and must confess that they are sinners, that is quite different than confessing all of our sins.

It is imperative that the believer confess his sins before the Lord. This is an acknowledgment that he has sinned, that he is in the wrong, and that he needs the mercy and grace of God. Man's problem is sin, and the only solution for it is Jesus Christ and Him crucified, i.e., the Cross.

Please understand that when we speak of the believer confessing sin, we aren't meaning that he has to go to a church, call a preacher, etc., in order to do such. In fact, all he has to do is, in his heart—without even saying anything—tell the Lord, "I have sinned," whatever the sin might be, and ask the Lord to forgive him. It's just that simple. It's not a ritual, and it's not a ceremony. It's an admittance which the Lord demands:

"Against You, You only, have I sinned, and done this evil in Your sight: that You might be justified when You speak, and be clear when You judge. (While David's sins were against Bath-sheba, her husband Uriah, and all of Israel, still, the ultimate direction of sin, perfected by Satan, is always against God. All sin is a departure from God's ways to man's ways. David is saying that God is always 'justified' in any action that He takes, and His 'judgment' is always perfect.) (The Expositor's Study Bible).

SIN

"Behold, I was shaped in iniquity; and in sin did my mother conceive me. (Unequivocally, this verse proclaims the fact of

original sin. This passage states that all are born in sin, and as a result of Adam's fall in the garden of Eden. "When Adam, as the federal head of the human race, failed, this means that all of humanity failed. It means that all who would be born would, in effect, be born lost)" (Ps. 51:4-5).

That's the reason that Jesus had to be born of a virgin. If man had anything to do with Mary's pregnancy, this would mean that Jesus had been born in original sin like everyone else. So, it was absolutely imperative that He be born, but He had to be born of a virgin exactly as prophesied some 750 years earlier by the great Prophet Isaiah (Isa. 7:14).

Without a doubt, this prophecy given by Isaiah is one of the greatest, if not the greatest, in the Bible.

In Hebrew, the word virgin is *haalmah,* which means "the virgin—the only one that ever was or ever will be a mother in this way."

The son who would be born would be the *"Son of God."* The word *Immanuel* means "God with us." Such was fulfilled in Christ.

This prophecy was given by God as a rebuttal to the efforts of Satan working through the kings of Syria and Israel to unseat Ahaz. In other words, their efforts to make void the promise of God given to David would come to naught.

THE FALL

As a result of the fall of Adam and Eve in the garden of Eden, the second man, the last Adam, the Lord Jesus Christ, had to come into this world, in effect, God becoming man, to undo what the original Adam did. He would have to keep the law of God perfectly, which He did, all as our substitute. Then He would have to pay the penalty for the terrible sin debt owed by all of mankind, for all have broken the law. This He did by giving Himself on the Cross of Calvary (Jn. 3:16).

To escape the judgment of original sin, man must be "born again," which is carried out by the believing sinner expressing faith in Christ and what Christ did for us at the Cross (Jn. 3:3; Eph. 2:8-9).

TRUTH

Behold, You desire truth in the inward parts: and in the hidden part You shall make me to know wisdom (man can only deal with the externals, and even that not very well; God alone can deal with the 'inward parts' of man, which is the source of sin, which speaks of the heart; in other words, the heart (the soul and the spirit) has to be changed, which the Lord alone can do [Mat. 5:8]). *Purge me with hyssop, and I shall be clean: wash me, and I shall be whiter than snow.* (The petition, 'purge me with hyssop,' expresses a figure of speech. 'Purge me with the blood which on that night in Egypt was sprinkled on the doorposts with a bunch of hyssop' [Ex. 12:13, 22] portrays David's dependence on 'the blood of the Lamb.' David had no recourse in the Law, even as no one has recourse in the Law. The Law can only condemn. All recourse is found exclusively in Christ and what He did for us at the Cross, of which the slain lamb and the blood on the doorposts in Egypt were symbols [Ex. 12:13; Ps. 51:1-7])(Ps. 51:6-7) (The Expositor's Study Bible).

Everyone who is saved is dependent solely and wholly on Christ and His sacrificial offering of Himself, and not at all upon our own personal merit, good works, etc. It has always been, it is, and it ever shall be *Jesus Christ and Him crucified* (I Cor. 1:23).

THE WORD OF THE LORD

He in the first year of his reign, in the first month, opened the doors of the house of the LORD, *and repaired them. And he brought in the priests and the Levites, and gathered them together into the east street, and said unto them, Hear Me, you Levites, sanctify now yourselves, and sanctify the house of the* LORD *God of your fathers, and carry forth the filthiness out of the holy place. For our fathers have trespassed, and done that which was evil in the eyes of the* LORD *our God, and have forsaken Him, and have turned away their faces from the habitation of the* LORD, *and turned their backs. Also they have shut up the doors of the porch, and put out the lamps, and have not burned incense nor offered burnt offerings in the holy place unto the God of Israel. Wherefore the wrath of the* LORD *was upon Judah and Jerusalem, and He has delivered them to trouble, to astonishment, and to hissing, as you see with your eyes. For, lo, our fathers have fallen by the sword, and our sons and our daughters and our wives are in captivity for this. Now it is in my heart to make a covenant with the LORD God of Israel, that His fierce wrath may turn away from us. My sons, be not now negligent: for the LORD has chosen you to stand before Him, to serve Him, and that you should minister unto Him, and burn incense* (II Chron. 29:3-11).

REPENTENCE

Immediately upon becoming king, Hezekiah began to institute reform. He wasted no time! Under his evil father Ahaz, the doors to the house of the Lord had been closed, meaning that this house was no longer in use. He quickly began to repair things.

In our own spiritual lives, how much presently needs repairing?

The word *sanctify* (or sanctification) of verse 5 simply means in this case, "to set apart for the exclusive use of God." In doing this, the filthiness would be carried out of the Holy Place.

Regarding our lives, when given the opportunity, the Holy Spirit will always clean us up. Paul said, *"Let us cleanse ourselves from all filthiness of the flesh and spirit, perfecting holiness in the fear of God"* (II Cor. 7:1).

THE COVENANT

Repentance alone could reverse the situation of Judah. This means turning back to the Cross, for the Cross alone can address sin (Heb. 10:12). Let it be quickly stated that humanistic psychology holds no answer whatsoever, and let it also be stated that one cannot have both. If the Cross of Christ, which is the only answer, is embraced, humanistic psychology and all such foolishness have to go. Conversely, if humanistic psychology is embraced, the Cross of Christ has to go. One cannot have both. One will either hate the one, and love the other; or else he will hold to the one, and despise the other. One cannot serve God and mammon.

The golden lampstand situated in the Holy Place of the temple typified Christ as the Light of the World. It had long since gone out! The burning of incense typified the intercession of Christ, all on our behalf. The burnt offerings typified the Cross, where the perfection of Christ is given to the believing sinner. The judgment was obvious! Because the temple was symbolic of Christ and the Cross, when Christ and the Cross are forsaken, judgment is inevitable! There can be no other way.

Sin puts people in captivity, even as verse 9 proclaims, and it also kills.

The covenant of verse 10 meant simply to obey the Word of God.

THE REPAIRING OF THE DOORS

Hezekiah waited no time at all in getting started regarding the work that needed to be done. The Scripture says, *"He in the first year of his reign, in the first month, opened the doors of the house of the LORD, and repaired them"* (II Chron. 29:3).

Work of this nature that must be done for the Lord cannot tolerate delay. It must begin immediately. The Scripture plainly tells us, *"Today if you will hear His voice, harden not your hearts"* (Heb. 4:7). Procrastination regarding the things of God proclaims a sure road to ruin. Hezekiah began immediately because the need was immediate, and he responded accordingly.

All of this means that there's no time like the present to get things right with God. To wait will always produce a catastrophe; to function immediately will always find the Lord helping such an individual.

THE CONSECRATION OF HEZEKIAH

Considering that Hezekiah's father, Ahaz, was one of the most wicked men to grace the throne of Judah, and realizing that Ahaz surely did not steer his son toward the Lord, we have to wonder at this man's consecration.

The great Prophet Isaiah could very well have been instrumental in the direction taken by the young king. The Scripture says concerning Isaiah, *"The vision of Isaiah the son of Amoz, which he saw concerning Judah and Jerusalem in the days of Uzziah, Jotham, Ahaz, and Hezekiah, kings of Judah"* (Isa. 1:1).

Isaiah was a contemporary of the prophets Jonah, Amos, Hosea, and Micah. It is thought that he began to preach at about 15 years of age and died at about 85. Tradition says that Manasseh, incensed over the preaching of Isaiah, placed the great prophet in a hollow log and cut him in two (Heb. 11:37). The great book which bears his name was written about 800 years before Christ.

His prophecies covered the entire or the partial reign of some four kings as listed in the text. Every message was primarily related to Judah, Jerusalem, or to the Jews and their Holy City.

REPAIR

Isaiah is called "the millennial prophet," having given more prophecies concerning that coming grand day than any other prophet. As well, he was quoted by Christ more than any other prophet. What an honor!

Of the four kings under whom Isaiah prophesied, Hezekiah was the godliest (Isa. 1:1).

One thing is certain: Ahaz gave no credence at all to the great Prophet Isaiah. Obviously, his son Hezekiah did!

Evidently the doors of the temple were in a state of disrepair. Seemingly, this would be the first thing that would be repaired. Incidentally, these "doors" were a type of Christ.

Jesus said concerning this:

"Verily, verily, I say unto you, I am the door of the sheep ('I am,' exclusive of all others! there is only 'one door,' and that 'door' is Christ)."

JESUS

All who ever came before Me are thieves and robbers (pertains to any and all before or after Christ, who claim to have the way of salvation without Christ!)*: but the sheep did not hear them* (true sheep cannot be deceived). *I am the door* (presents an emphatic statement; the church is not the door to Christ as the Catholics teach, but Christ is the door to the church): *by Me if any man enter in, he shall be saved* (as the 'door,' Jesus is the 'Saviour'), *and shall go in and out, and find pasture* (they went in for safety and went out for pasture) (Jn. 10:7-9) (The Expositor's Study Bible).

In one way or the other, everything about the temple pointed to Christ in His atoning, mediatorial, or intercessory work. This is so important, let us say it again: Jesus Christ is the door to all the things of God, and He is that door by virtue of the Cross. In other words, He is the source of all things from God, and the Cross is the means by which these things are given to us, all superintended by the Holy Spirit (Rom. 8:1-2, 11).

JESUS CHRIST IS THE NEW COVENANT

Everything about the new covenant—the greatest legislation, if one would refer to such in that capacity, that has ever been given to mankind—is all in Christ. It has no temple, no altars—that is, as it regards sacrifices—no ceremonies, and no rituals, only Christ.

A covenant is always between two or more people. If either one or either side breaks the covenant, the results are meant to be terrible. Contrary to all covenants, even though the new covenant is between God and man, still, it cannot fail because it is all in Christ. Christ is both God and man, the second man, and as He is both, it is all in Him, and it cannot fail. Man may fail, but Christ will never fail, so that means the covenant will never fail; hence, it can be referred to as the *"everlasting covenant"* (Heb. 13:20).

So, if anything is going to truly be done for God, Jesus Christ had better be the first and the last, the all in all, the King of kings and Lord of lords!

SANCTIFY YOURSELVES

The word *sanctify*, or *sanctification*, simply means "to set apart from something to something;" in this case, from the world unto the Lord, and exclusively unto the Lord.

Sanctification before the Cross was little more than an external affair. It had to be that way due to the fact that the Holy Spirit did not then abide in the hearts and lives of believers. He was with believers but not in believers as He is presently (Jn. 14:17-18).

Before the Cross, sanctification referred to anything and everything that was not strictly according to the law of Moses. Such particulars, whatever they might have been, had to be addressed. That pretty much concluded the sanctification process.

Since the Cross, the Holy Spirit comes into the heart and life of the believer, there to abide forever (Jn. 14:16); consequently, sanctification presently has nothing to do with the law and everything to do with grace.

Under the new covenant, it's not possible for the believer to sanctify himself, other than make himself available to the Holy Spirit.

THE HOLY SPIRIT

The modern believer, which refers to all since the Cross, is to place his or her faith exclusively in Christ and what Christ has done for us at the Cross. The Holy Spirit, who works exclusively within the parameters of the finished work of Christ, will then begin to develop His fruit within one's heart and life, which means that one is then set apart from the world unto God.

The believer must understand that he can have the *"fruit of the Spirit"* only as long as he places his faith exclusively in Christ and the Cross. This is because the Holy Spirit works exclusively within the parameters of the finished work of Christ and, in fact, will work according to no other manner (Rom. 8:1-11; Eph. 2:13-18).

If the believer takes another tactic, he will come up with *"works of the flesh."*

Actually, the fruit of the Spirit and the works of the flesh are addressed by the Holy Spirit through Paul in the same chapter of Galatians (Gal. 5:19-23). In effect, the Holy Spirit is saying that it's going to be one or the other as it regards the believer. If the believer tries to live this life by means other than the Cross of Christ, as stated, the works of the flesh will be the end result. If faith is properly placed in the Cross of Christ, the end result will be the development of the fruit of the Spirit.

The fruit of the Spirit, as stated, is the result of sanctification, while the works of the flesh are the result of self-will.

LAMPS, INCENSE, AND BURNT OFFERINGS

The golden lampstands in the temple typified the mediato-rial work of Christ. The burning of incense, which was carried out twice a day, 9 AM and 3 PM, was meant to typify the inter-cessory work of Christ, all on our behalf. Of course, the burnt offerings typified Calvary and, therefore, the atonement. So, in these three particulars, we have the entirety of the work of Christ—atonement, mediator, and intercessor.

Under King Ahaz, all of this had ceased. As a result, *"The wrath of the LORD was upon Judah and Jerusalem."*

As we have said elsewhere in this volume, the only thing standing between mankind and the judgment of God is the Cross of Christ. That's why it is imperative that preachers preach the Cross and that believers place their faith exclusively in the Cross of Christ.

The Cross of Christ is as necessary to the believer as oxygen is to our breathing. If the Cross of Christ is ignored or laid aside, or unbelief is tendered toward this greatest of the work of Christ, judgment in the form of the wrath of God is the end result.

When Hezekiah instituted these reforms and cried to God for a revival, Judah was in a terrible state; likewise, the present church is in a terrible state. It may even be that the modern church is in worse shape than Judah of old. At least Judah knew the difference in right and wrong. The modern church seems to have little understanding anymore as to what is right or what is wrong.

CHURCHES

One might say that there are basically four classes of churches in Christendom. They are as follows:

1. Modernist churches, which do not believe the Bible, that Jesus is the Son of God, or that Calvary effected anything.

2. Churches that claim to believe in the atoning work of Calvary but completely ignore it.

3. Churches that claim to preach the Cross, but instead, preach psychology, the greed gospel, or something else.

4. Churches that preach "Jesus Christ and Him crucified" as the foundation of all faith. Sadly, these are few and far between.

THE LEVITES

Then the Levites arose, Mahath the son of Amasai, and Joel the son of Azariah, of the sons of the Kohathites: and of the sons of Merari, Kish the son of Abdi, and Azariah the son of Jehalelel: and of the Gershonites; Joah the son of Zimmah, and Eden the son of Joah: And of the sons of Elizaphan; Shimri, and Jeiel: and of the sons of Asaph; Zechariah, and Mattaniah: And of the sons of Heman; Jehiel, and Shimei: and of the sons of Jeduthun; Shemaiah, and Uzziel. And they gathered their brethren, and sanctified themselves, and came, according to the commandment of the king, by the words of the Lord, *to cleanse the house of the* Lord. *And the priests went into the inner part of the house of the* Lord, *to cleanse it, and brought out all the uncleanness that they found in the temple of the* Lord *into the court of the house of the* Lord. *And the Levites took it, to carry it out abroad into the brook Kidron. Now they began on the first day of the first month to sanctify, and on the eighth day of the month came they to the porch of the* Lord: *so they sanctified the house of the* Lord *in eight days; and in the sixteenth day of the first month they made an end. Then they went in to Hezekiah the king, and said, We have cleansed all the house of the* Lord, *and the altar of burnt offering, with all the vessels thereof, and the shewbread table, with all the vessels thereof. Moreover all the vessels, which King Ahaz in his reign did cast away in his transgression, have we prepared and sanctified, and behold, they are before the altar of the* Lord (II Chron. 29:12-19).

THE INNER PART

The names of the 14 Levites given in these passages have no interest for the historians of the world, but such an interest for the Holy Spirit that they are all set out here. They have been read already by hundreds of millions of people for nearly 2,800 years.

The words or commands of the Lord mentioned in verse 15 are such as are written in Exodus 19:22 and Leviticus 11:44.

Nothing can be spiritually cleansed unless it is done according to the Word of the Lord.

Only the priest could enter the temple, while the Levites' sphere of work and service lay in the courts and roundabout the temple.

Spiritually, revival must begin in the *"inner part,"* which means "the heart." It is unthinkable that the temple was in this condition, but sadly, it was. Is it possible that the modern church is in the same condition now as the temple of old?

The first thing that happens when a move of God begins to take place is that things are cleaned up, as recorded in verses 18 and 19.

TO CLEANSE THE HOUSE OF THE LORD

Under the new covenant, the believer is the *"house of the* LORD." Paul said, *"Know you not that you are the temple of God* (where the Holy Spirit abides), *and that the Spirit of God dwells in you?* (That makes the born-again believer His permanent home)" (I Cor. 3:16) (The Expositor's Study Bible).

The old covenant consisted, as is obvious, of carrying trash out of the temple and, at the same time, setting up the sacred vessels so they could be put immediately to use. Presently, under the new covenant, the cleansing of the house is totally different.

As already stated, the temple is no more, and the house is now the born-again believer. The Holy Spirit is the only one who can do the cleansing that is now required.

THE HOLY SPIRIT AND THE
CLEANSING OF THE TEMPLE

The Holy Spirit is God. Everything He does is done within the parameters, so to speak, of the finished work of Christ, i.e., the Cross. In other words, it is the Cross of Christ that has given the Holy Spirit the legal means to do all that He does with us (Rom. 8:2).

The Holy Spirit comes into our hearts and lives to abide, and to do so permanently, to carry out a great work. However, the greatest of all that He does is to rid the believer of the dominion of the sin nature. How is that done?

It is required of us (Rom. 8:2) that our faith ever be in Christ and what He did for us at the Cross. With that being done and maintained, and without fail, the Holy Spirit will then work mightily on our behalf. It is the Cross of Christ that gave and gives the legal means to the Holy Spirit to do all that He does.

Let me explain further: Before the Cross, the sacrificial system consisted of animal blood, which was woefully insufficient to take away sins (Heb. 10:4). So, this limited the Holy Spirit as to what He could do with each believer simply because the sin debt was still there. To be sure, the Holy Spirit was with believers during those times, but not in believers. While He did go into the hearts and lives of some few, such as prophets and some godly kings, to help them carry out their assigned tasks, when that was finished, He would then depart. However, since the Cross, the Holy Spirit comes into the heart and life of the believer, there to abide permanently (Jn. 14:16-17).

The great mistake that the believer makes is to take the Holy Spirit for granted. In other words, not understanding the Cross as it relates to the Holy Spirit, believers simply do not know or understand how the Holy Spirit works. They do not understand at all the part the Cross of Christ plays in all of this, which is a consummate part, to say the least.

DOMINION AND THE SIN NATURE

The sin nature is the human nature that has become corrupted. This took place at the fall of Adam when he fell from the lofty position of total God-consciousness down to the far, far lower level of total self-consciousness. All of this means that the very nature of the person—and we speak of one who is unredeemed—is altogether toward sin and transgression. In other words, the sin nature controls such a person 24 hours a day, seven days a week. Everything that is done lends toward sin, iniquity, transgression, self-will, etc. Even the so-called good things done have an ulterior motive. When the believing sinner comes to Christ, the sin nature is made dormant, i.e., ineffective (Rom. 6:6).

Sooner or later, the new convert fails the Lord in some way. This comes as a shock, but it has happened to every one of us. This does not within itself reactivate the sin nature. What reactivates it is because of the following: To try to keep from committing this sin again, whatever it may have been, the believer, either through ignorance or rebellion (it's almost always through ignorance), places his or her faith in something other than the

Cross of Christ. When this is done, the Holy Spirit cannot function, and that means that the sin nature will be reactivated and will begin to control or rule the believer in some way. That's what Paul was talking about when he said:

"Let not sin (the sin nature) *therefore reign* (rule) *in your mortal body* (showing that the sin nature can once again rule in the heart and life of the believer if the believer doesn't constantly look to Christ and the Cross; the 'mortal body' is neutral, which means it can be used for righteousness or unrighteousness), *that you should obey it in the lusts thereof* (ungodly lusts are carried out through the mortal body if faith is not maintained in the Cross" (Rom. 6:12) (The Expositor's Study Bible).

THE PHYSICAL BODY

Neither yield you your members (of your mortal body) *as instruments of unrighteousness unto sin* (the sin nature)*: but yield yourselves unto God* (we are to yield ourselves to Christ and the Cross; that alone guarantees victory over the sin nature), *as those who are alive from the dead* (we have been raised with Christ in 'newness of life'), *and your members as instruments of righteousness unto God* (this can be done only by virtue of the Cross and our faith in that finished work, and faith which continues in that finished work from day-to-day [Lk. 9:23-24]) (Rom. 6:13) (The Expositor's Study Bible).

If the believer doesn't place his faith exclusively in the Cross of Christ, the sin nature is going to rule such a believer in some way. This makes life miserable and is the very opposite of what the Holy Spirit intends (Rom. 7:19).

Virtually the entirety of the body of Christ, and we speak of consecrated Christians, is presently being ruled by the sin nature in some way. How do I know that?

I know that because the modern church is not preaching the Cross, and there is no other means or way of victory. It is the Cross of Christ, or it is law, and Paul said concerning this, *"But that no man is justified by the Law in the sight of God, it is evident"* (Gal. 3:11).

The great apostle also said, *"For as many as are of the works of the law are under the curse* (the believer can only be under law or grace; it is one or the other; one can only come to grace through the Cross; if one is trusting in law, whatever kind of law, one is cursed)*"* (Gal. 3:10). It doesn't matter if it's the law of Moses, laws that preachers have concocted, or laws we have concocted ourselves. Let us say it again: whatever kind of law it is, if it's not grace through the Cross, one is cursed.

WHAT DOES IT MEAN TO BE CURSED?

Now, please understand that we are speaking here of believers, not unbelievers. For believers to live in a state of being cursed is trouble indeed! And yet, that's where most believers presently are. They are living a cursed life, which means that the rudiments of Christianity—what it ought to be, and what it is meant to be—escape such a person. And yet, let me say it again: this is where virtually all modern believers are.

Why?

The reason is obvious. The only defense against being cursed is the Cross of Christ.

Regrettably, the modern church is not preaching the Cross. Most believers, and I speak of those who are truly born again, understand the Cross to a degree as it regards salvation, but have no understanding whatsoever as it regards sanctification. In other words, they don't know how we live for God on a daily basis, how we order our behavior, or how we have victory over the world, the flesh, and the Devil. Please understand that God has only one solution for this problem, and that is the Cross. However, by not understanding the Cross relative to sanctification, such a believer lives a life of spiritual failure, i.e., being cursed.

To be cursed means that the believer cannot live above sin. His spiritual life is one of constant failure. It is a constant round of sinning and repenting, sinning and repenting.

All of this brings on oppression, nervous disorders, and certain types of sickness, in other words, the very opposite of what living for God ought to be. It's all because of not understanding the Cross and not having faith in Christ and the Cross, which places one under a curse, and keeps one under a curse. This is a terrible way to have to live and is certainly not what the Lord intends.

Most believers do not understand that it was the Apostle Paul who gave us these great truths as it regards dominion over the sin nature, which means that we are no longer under the curse. In fact, I would say that over 99 percent of all of Paul's teaching was on this very subject. He gave a few Scriptures telling people how to be saved, but virtually everything was geared toward telling believers how to live for God.

That's the reason that many Christians say, once they've heard the Message of the Cross, and they have begun to embrace this all-important truth, "Brother Swaggart, I feel like I have just been born again again." It's a strange statement, but it is true. I know exactly how they feel. The Cross of Christ sets the captive free, at least if our faith is properly placed.

FAITH

It's not enough to merely have faith. One must have faith in the correct object, and what do we mean by that?

Most Christians have what I call a "shotgun faith." It really aims at nothing and just sort of scatters itself. While it may be faith, it's not faith that God will honor. The only faith that God will honor is faith in Christ and what Christ has done for us at the Cross. Some would quickly add, "But Brother Swaggart, my faith is in the Word of God. Isn't that where it's supposed to be?"

That is most definitely where it's supposed to be but please read the following very carefully: The entirety of the story of the Bible, and I mean its entirety, all the way from Genesis 1:1 through Revelation 22:21 is the story of "Jesus Christ and Him crucified." That's what the whole thing is all about. So, when you have faith in Christ and what He has done for us at the Cross, you are having faith in the Word of God; otherwise, you aren't. Please note the following very carefully:

- Jesus Christ is the source of all things we receive from God (Jn. 1:1-3, 14, 29; 14:6).

- The Cross of Christ is the only means by which we receive all of these wonderful things from God (Rom. 6:1-14; Col. 2:10-15).

- With Christ as the source and the Cross as the means, the Cross of Christ must ever be the object of our faith (I Cor. 1:17, 18, 23; 2:2; Gal. 6:14).

- With all of this being done—Christ as the source, the Cross as the means, and our faith planted in the Cross of Christ—the Holy Spirit will then begin to work on our behalf as only He can do, giving us daily victory over the world, the flesh, and the Devil (Rom. 8:1-11; Eph. 2:13-18).

DOMINION

The Bible does not teach sinless perfection; however, it does teach that sin is not to have dominion over us (Rom. 6:14).

Dominion of sin consists of a bondage (or bondages) of some sort that controls the individual. Regrettably, millions of Christians are plagued with the dominion of the sin nature. The believer can be free from this dominion only by the believer placing his or her faith exclusively in Christ and the Cross, which then gives the Holy Spirit latitude to work within our lives, bringing about the desired results. Still, this does not mean that the believer is totally free from committing acts of sin at times.

The Scripture says, *"For all have sinned* (presents all men placed in the same category), *and come short of the glory of God* (the Greek text implies that even the most Righteous among us continue to come short of the Glory of God on a continuing basis)" (Rom. 3:23) (The Expositor's Study Bible).

Sinless perfection will not be reached until the trump of God sounds. The Scripture says concerning this, *"For this corruptible* (sin nature) *must put on incorruption* (a Glorified Body with no sin nature), *and this mortal* (subject to death) *must put on immortality* (will never die)" (I Cor. 15:53) (The Expositor's Study Bible).

As stated, it is the business now of the Holy Spirit to clean up the child of God, and this He will do if the believer will only cooperate with Him by placing his or her faith exclusively in the finished work of Christ and leaving it there.

THE ALTAR OF THE LORD

Concerning the temple, the altar was the great brazen altar, some 30 feet wide and 30 feet long. It sat immediately in front of the temple and was where the sacrifices of every nature were offered. It symbolized Calvary in all of its forms. In fact, one might say that the *"altar of the LORD"* was the most significant vessel in the entirety of the temple apparatus.

Immediately, one may counter by saying that the ark of the covenant was the most important vessel. In the strict sense of the word, that is correct; however, there was only one who could enter the Holy of Holies, and we speak of the high priest. He could enter only once a year, and then, not without blood, which means that a sacrifice had to be first offered on the *"altar of the LORD."* The blood of that sacrifice was then taken and sprinkled on the mercy seat in the Holy of Holies, which was on the Great Day of Atonement.

THE WORK OF THE ALTAR

The great altar was in use 24 hours a day, seven days a week. In fact, it had four horns, one at each corner, symbolizing that redemption was the same the world over. This means that the gospel is not a white man's gospel, a red man's gospel, etc., but is the gospel for the entirety of the world (Jn. 3:16).

The fires on the great altar were to be kept burning 24 hours a day, seven days a week, for the simple reason that the people were constantly bringing sacrifices to be offered. In other words, the work of the great altar was never finished and, as well, operated, so to speak, around the clock. And yet, the millions of sacrifices offered throughout some 15 centuries could not equal the one sacrifice of Christ. The Scripture says, *"For by one offering He has perfected forever them who are sanctified"* (Heb. 10:14).

THE SACRIFICES

Then Hezekiah the king rose early, and gathered the rulers of the city, and went up to the house of the LORD. And they brought seven bullocks, and seven rams, and seven lambs, and seven he goats, for a sin offering for the kingdom, and for the sanctuary, and for Judah. And he commanded the priests the sons of Aaron to offer them on the altar of the LORD. So they killed the bullocks, and the priests received the blood, and sprinkled it on the altar: likewise, when they had killed the rams, they sprinkled the blood upon the altar: they killed also the lambs, and they sprinkled the blood upon the altar. And they brought forth the he goats for the sin offering before the king and the congregation; and they laid their hands upon them: And the priests killed them, and they made reconciliation with their blood upon the altar, to make an atonement for all Israel: for the king commanded that the burnt offering and the sin offering should be made for all Israel (II Chron. 29:20-24).

SEVEN

After the cleansing of the temple, which made it serviceable, the first thing that was now done, in essence, was that Judah went back to the Cross. I must believe that the Holy Spirit urged Hezekiah to institute seven sacrifices of each of the various animals. *Seven* signifies perfection, universality, and totality. It is God's number. It means that Israel was to have a complete cleansing. While the temple could be cleansed of debris, it took the shed blood of the lamb to properly cleanse from sin. We as believers can prepare the way, but only the blood can cleanse (I Jn. 1:7).

The sprinkling of the blood marked the expiation of sin (Lev. 4:7, 18, 30; 5:9; 8:14-15; Heb. 9:12-14, 19-22).

The laying of the hands on the head of the animal signified the transferring of the sins of the person offering the sacrifice—in this case, the entirety of the people of Judah—to the victim, which was a type of Christ taking our sins on the Cross (Isa. 53:6). This is that of which Paul was speaking when he mentioned the *"laying on of hands"* in Hebrews 6:2.

The burnt offering typified Christ giving His perfection to the sinner. The sin offering typified the sinner giving his sin to Christ. He gives His perfection to us; we give our sins to Him.

THE SIN OFFERING

Four particular animals— seven each—were offered:

- Seven bullocks
- Seven rams
- Seven lambs
- Seven he goats

All of these were for a sin offering. As we have stated, the sin offering portrayed the believing sinner giving his sin to Christ. In this case, the priests laid their hands on the heads of these animals, and in doing so, confessed the sins of Judah, which were many.

After the hands were laid on the heads of these animals, *"the priests killed them."* This, of course, typified the death of Christ on the Cross. He gave up His life, a perfect life, by the means of a perfect body, as a sacrifice that was accepted by God.

THE SPRINKLING OF THE BLOOD

When the animals were killed by their throats being slit, the blood was caught in a basin, and then it was sprinkled upon the altar. This was the first time in years this had been done. Now, that which typified the great price that Christ would pay at Calvary was once again instituted. True revival always leads the church to Calvary—every time to Calvary.

Judah's protection was the shed blood of the lamb! Her prosperity was the shed blood of the lamb! Her healing was the shed blood of the lamb! All forgiveness of sins was by the shed blood of the lamb!

Please understand that it hasn't changed from then until now and, in fact, will never change. Every iota of faith must be exclusively in the Cross of Christ. While other things have their place, the great foundation principle of the redemption plan, i.e., the new covenant, has always been, is, and ever shall be the shed blood of the Lamb!

THE WORSHIP OF THE LORD

And He set the Levites in the house of the LORD with cymbals, with psalteries, and with harps, according to the commandment of David, and of Gad the king's seer, and Nathan the prophet: for so was the commandment of the LORD by His prophets. And the Levites stood with the instruments of David, and the priests with the trumpets. And Hezekiah commanded to offer the burnt offering upon the altar. And when the burnt offering began, the song of the LORD began also with the trumpets, and with the instruments ordained by David king of Israel. And all the congregation worshipped, and the singers sang, and the trumpeters sounded: and all this continued until the burnt offering was finished. And when they had made an end of offering, the king and all who were present with him bowed themselves, and worshipped. Moreover Hezekiah the king and the princes commanded the Levites to sing praise unto the LORD with the words of David, and of Asaph the seer. And they sang praises with gladness, and they bowed their heads and worshipped (II Chron. 29:25-30).

THE WORSHIP OF THE LORD
WITH MUSIC AND SINGING

Music and joy always accompany faith in the Cross because all sins have been washed away.

The Bible does not distinguish between a seer and prophet. Sometimes both designations are used for the same individual (I Chron. 21:9; II Chron. 29:25).

When faith is properly placed in Christ and the Cross, worship always follows as it regards music and singing. No Cross, no worship; little Cross, little worship; much Cross, much worship!

From all of this, it is obvious that Hezekiah was doing his very best to set the house in order exactly as the Lord had given it to David so long before. He called in the musicians and the singers, and it was campmeeting time, so to speak!

We learn from this just how significant that music and singing are as it regards the worship of the Lord. In fact, I think one could say without fear of exaggeration that it is the highest form of worship.

THE PSALMS

We learn this from the great book of Psalms. It is the longest book in the Bible, meaning that the Holy Spirit designated the greatest amount of space to praise and worship with music and singing. That speaks volumes! That's the reason that Satan has done everything within hell's power to pervert the worship of the Lord regarding music and singing. Regrettably, he has succeeded in many, if not most, cases. The Evil One knows how tremendously significant that proper music and singing actually are.

When I was 8 years of age, I asked the Lord to give me the talent to play the piano. The Lord heard my prayer and not only gave me that talent but, as well, gave me an understanding of what the Holy Spirit wants and desires as it regards the worship of the Lord through music and singing. He has helped me to touch the world for Christ by the means of music and singing, for which we give the Lord all the praise and all the glory.

Seeing what Hezekiah has done, we can only say, "Happy days are here again."

SACRIFICES

> *Then Hezekiah answered and said, Now you have consecrated yourselves unto the LORD, come near and bring sacrifices and thank offerings into the house of the LORD. And the congregation brought in sacrifices and thank offerings; and as many as were of a free heart burnt offerings. And the number of the burnt offerings, which the congregation brought, was threescore and ten bullocks, an hundred rams, and two hundred lambs: all these were for a burnt offering to the LORD. And the consecrated things were six hundred oxen and three thousand sheep. But the priests were too few, so that they could not flay all the burnt offerings: wherefore their brethren the Levites did help them, till the work was ended, and until the other priests had sanctified themselves: for the Levites were more upright in heart to sanctify themselves than the priests. And also the burnt offerings were in abundance, with the fat of the peace offerings, and the drink offerings for every burnt offering. So the service of the house of the LORD was set in order. And Hezekiah rejoiced, and all the people, that God had prepared the people: for the thing was done suddenly* (II Chron. 29:31-36).

With the opening of the temple, the people of Judah sang *"praise unto the LORD with the words of David, and of Asaph the seer."*

The drink offerings poured out on the altar signified Christ pouring out His life on the Cross. The Scripture says, *"The thing was done suddenly,"* meaning that Hezekiah felt a great urgency to cleanse the temple in order that the sacrifices may begin, and rightly so!

THE CROSS OF CALVARY

As the people began to sing praises unto the Lord, thousands of animals would be offered up in sacrifice, proclaiming the fact that Judah's safety and protection, her power and strength, her prosperity, and, in fact, all good things had their foundation in the Cross of Calvary. Of course, the blood of bulls and goats could never take away sins, but faith registered in what it all represented guaranteed salvation and the blessings of God.

In 1997, the Lord began to give me a revelation of the Cross, which has revolutionized my life, my ministry, and all things that pertain to the Lord. No, it isn't new, having been given to the apostle Paul nearly 2,000 years ago. However, as far as most of the modern church is concerned, it is most definitely new because it has been decades since the Cross has been preached in most churches.

In fact, the foundation of the Cross was actually laid down by the Godhead from before the foundation of the world. That means this is the oldest doctrine in the entirety of the Bible (I Pet. 1:18-20). It also means that every single Bible doctrine is built on the Message of the Cross; otherwise, it is spurious. As a result, the modern church hardly knows anymore exactly what the gospel actually is. The reason? Very simply, they have little understanding of the Cross of Christ, especially as it regards our sanctification (I Cor. 1:17).

Jesus has died and has risen again,
Pardon and peace to bestow;
Fully I trust Him; from sin's guilty stain,
Jesus saves me now.

Sin's condemnation is over and gone,
Jesus alone knows how;
Life and salvation my soul has put on:
Jesus saves me now.

Satan may tempt, but he shall never reign,
That Christ will never allow;
Doubts I have buried,
And this is my strain,
Jesus saves me now.

Resting in Jesus, abiding in Him,
Gladly my faith can avow,
Never again need my pathway be dim,
Jesus saves me now.

Jesus is stronger than Satan and sin,
Satan to Jesus must bow;
Therefore I triumphed
Without and within;
Jesus saves me now.

Sorrow and pain may beset me about,
Nothing can darken my brow;
Battling in faith I can joyfully shout:
"Jesus saves me now."

HEZEKIAH

CHAPTER 2

THE PASSOVER

THE PASSOVER

"And Hezekiah sent to all Israel and Judah, and wrote letters also to Ephraim and Manasseh, that they should come to the house of the Lord at Jerusalem, to keep the Passover unto the Lord God of Israel. For the king had taken counsel, and his princes, and all the congregation in Jerusalem, to keep the Passover in the second month. For they could not keep it at that time, because the priests had not sanctified themselves sufficiently, neither had the people gathered themselves together to Jerusalem. And the thing pleased the king and all the congregation. So they established a decree to make proclamation throughout all Israel, from Beer-sheba even to Dan, that they should come to keep the Passover unto the Lord God of Israel at Jerusalem: for they had not done it of a long time in such sort as it was written" (II Chron. 30:1-5).

The Passover is a type of Calvary (Ex. 12:13). The Passover was supposed to be kept the first month (Ex. 12:2-3), but because of all the things that needed to be done, they would have to keep the Passover a month late, i.e., *"the second month"* (II Chron. 30:2).

Even though Israel was now divided, still, Hezekiah sent a message throughout both kingdoms, giving all an invitation to come and keep the Passover.

THE PASSOVER

The word *Passover* in the Hebrew is *Pesah* and comes from a verb meaning "to pass over," in the sense of "to spare" (Ex. 12:13, 27).

This affords excellent sense. There is no need to jettison the time-honored view that God literally passed over the blood-sprinkled Israelite houses while smiting those of the Egyptians. Of course, the Israelite houses had the blood applied to the doorposts as they were commanded to do.

Exodus 12:43-49 excluded Gentiles from partaking in the Passover unless they had become proselytes, who were expected, even obliged, to conform fully.

As it regarded the particulars of the Passover, a lamb was roasted and then eaten with unleavened bread and bitter herbs. The lamb was typical of Christ and what He would do at the Cross. The unleavened bread typified His perfection, and the bitter herbs typified the bitterness of the Cross.

In the case of Israel, the bitter herbs typified the bitterness of Egyptian bondage.

The symbolism, *"Christ our Passover,"* as given to us by Paul (I Cor. 5:7), in effect, specifies that the Passover was a type of

Christ and what He would do at the Cross in order to deliver humanity, at least for those who will believe.

How much the Jews understood this is anyone's guess. I suspect that their thinking was mostly upon the deliverance from Egyptian bondage; nevertheless, the Passover ritual was, and was intended to be, a type of the sacrifice of Christ.

THE CROSS OF CHRIST

At the time that Hezekiah issued his decree regarding the eating of the Passover, such had not been kept for *"a long time."* Consequently, it was imperative that Judah keep this all-important ritual.

The only thing that stands between the fierce anger of God and mankind is the blood of Jesus Christ, i.e., the Cross. Self-righteousness tends to think that surely God looks at all of our good works. He doesn't! He looks only at the precious shed blood of Jesus Christ and our faith in that sacrifice, that is, if we have faith. If the church does not preach and proclaim the blood, it preaches nothing that is of any value to its adherents. In fact, all the feast days of Israel, with their sacrifices and rituals, had as their foundation the Passover. Likewise, everything in the church must be tied to Calvary. Calvary must be the foundation, as it is truly the foundation. Our worship must spring from Calvary. Our prosperity must spring from Calvary. Our preaching must be Calvary-centered. No wonder Paul would say, *"I determined not to know anything among you save Jesus Christ, and Him crucified"* (I Cor. 2:2).

How many churches have the Cross as their foundation? Sadly, precious few!

GRACIOUS AND MERCIFUL

So the posts went with the letters from the king and his princes throughout all Israel and Judah, and according to the commandment of the king, saying, You children of Israel, turn again unto the Lord God of Abraham, Isaac, and Israel, and He will return to the remnant of you, who are escaped out of the hand of the kings of Assyria. And you be not like your fathers, and like your brethren, who trespassed against the Lord God of their fathers, who therefore gave them up to desolation, as you see. Now be you not stiffnecked, as your fathers were, but yield yourselves unto the Lord, and enter into His sanctuary, which He has sanctified forever: and serve the Lord your God, that the fierceness of His wrath may turn away from you. For if you turn again unto the Lord, your brethren and your children shall find compassion before them that lead them captive, so that they shall come again unto this land: for the Lord your God is gracious and merciful, and will not turn away His face from you, if you return unto Him (II Chron. 30:6-9).

THE WRATH OF GOD

The northern kingdom had fallen by now, and so Assyria had left the poorest of the poor in the land, with the elite taken out as captives; however, they were precious in God's sight just the same. Regrettably, as we shall sadly see, most would not take this opportunity offered by Hezekiah. The only thing that assuages the wrath of God is Calvary. His wrath will either be turned toward the unrepentant Christian or Calvary. The price of sin must be paid. If we accept the price that He paid at Calvary, then His wrath has already been expended toward His Son, the Lord Jesus Christ. If we do not accept the price that was paid at Calvary, then His wrath is turned toward us.

Verse 9 proclaims the fact—no doubt, given to Hezekiah by the Holy Spirit—that restoration was possible, but only if repentance was enjoined.

THE CROSS OF CHRIST

As we have stated, the only thing that assuages the anger of God and, thereby, the judgment of God against sin is Calvary.

Let us say it this way: The only thing standing between mankind and the wrath of God is the Cross of Christ. That's the reason the church is to ever hold up the Cross as the beacon of light for a darkened world. Regrettably and sadly, however, the modern church has long since, as a whole, ceased to preach the Cross. It is mentioned once in awhile in some churches as it regards salvation, but it is understood not at all as it regards sanctification, in other words, how we live for God, how we order our behavior, and how we obtain victory over the world, the flesh, and the Devil. That is sad when one considers that it was to Paul that the truth of the new covenant was given.

In fact, Jesus is the new covenant, but the Cross is the meaning of that new covenant, the meaning of which is the Cross of Christ. If we objectively look at Paul's writings, we find that virtually all of what he had to say, literally what was given to him by the Holy Spirit, was to believers. In other words, he was telling believers how to live for God.

HOW TO LIVE FOR GOD!

Sometime ago at Family Worship Center in our Wednesday night Bible study, I made the simple statement, "Most Christians simply do not know how to live for God." It's a simple statement, as is obvious, but it came as a shock to those who heard it. You could feel the tension in the auditorium.

To not know how to live for God is tantamount to spiritual failure, but the sadness is, most Christians simply do not understand how to live for God. Functioning in that capacity, believers go from one scheme to the other, in other words, the flavor of the month. How do I know that most believers don't know how to live for God?

I know simply because most believers have no idea whatsoever the part the Cross of Christ plays in the sanctification process, in other words, how we live for God. Not knowing that, what knowledge they do have really is error, which makes life difficult to say the least. To fully live for God, which means to fully enjoy more abundant life, means that we must understand the Cross of Christ as it regards our everyday walk before the Lord.

THE SIN NATURE

The following was given to us by the apostle Paul.

First of all, most Christians have no idea whatsoever as to what the sin nature really is.

The sin nature is that which came to all human beings through our original parent—Adam. When Adam fell, he fell from the position of total God-consciousness far down to the position of total self-consciousness. His very nature became that of sin. In other words, everything he did was sin, even that which seemed to be good. If looked at long enough, it would be found to be of ulterior motive. Such has passed on to every human being who has ever lived.

Isn't the sin nature removed at conversion?

No!

It is made dormant, meaning inactive, but it isn't removed.

Why is it that the Lord doesn't remove it at that time? The Lord has left such in our hearts and lives to serve as a disciplinary measure. In other words, we are meant to know and understand that if we try to function any way other than God's way, which is the Cross, the sin nature is going to rule us as believers, which will cause all types of problems.

In Chapter 6 of Romans, which is the chapter that explains the sin nature, Paul mentions sin some 17 times. Sixteen of those 17 times he is speaking of the sin nature. Only in verse 15 is he speaking of acts of sin. Now, how do I know that?

In the original text, he used in front of the word *sin* what is referred to as the definite article, making it read "*the* sin."

In other words, he was not talking about acts of sin, except in verse 15, but rather the sin nature. The reason the King James translators did not add the word *the* in these cases, and hundreds of other times in the New Testament, is because it is clumsy in English. Actually, in verse 14, he did not use the definite article; nevertheless, the word *sin* as used here is a noun, which means that he was still referring to the sin nature.

If there is no such thing as a sin nature, or else, it no longer is in the heart and life of the believer, then Paul spent an awful lot of time and space explaining something that doesn't exist. To be sure, the sin nature most definitely does exist. It will not be removed until the resurrection.

Paul said again: *"For this corruptible* (sin nature) *must put on incorruption"* (I Cor. 15:53). Then we will be rid of the sin nature forever, but until then, it's a problem with which we have to contend.

WHAT CAUSES THE SIN NATURE
TO BE REACTIVATED?

It's not necessarily sin that causes it to be reactivated, so to speak, but rather what we do with the sin. Where do we place our faith? If we try to overcome the problem by any means other than faith in Christ and the Cross, this will quickly reactivate the sin nature, which greatly hinders the Holy Spirit. The key to all victory for any and every believer is the Cross of Christ. When we speak of the Cross, we aren't speaking of the wooden beam on which Jesus died, but rather what He there accomplished.

When the believer places his faith in anything other than Christ and the Cross, the Holy Spirit through Paul labels such as *"the flesh."*

What is the flesh?

The flesh is that which constitutes what a human being can do. In other words, it's our education, motivation, talent, ability, willpower, etc. Those things within themselves aren't wrong; however, one cannot live for God by those means. It simply cannot be done, but yet, that's where most believers are. The flesh is very easily religionized, and with that being the case, it seems to be right when it's not.

Let us say it again: The believer must understand that it was at the Cross where all sin was atoned, and all victory was won. It's where we must place our faith. Then and only then will the sin nature be inactive.

EXACTLY WHAT IS THE SIN NATURE?

First of all, the sin nature is not something physical. It's not a physical organ of any nature. The sin nature is a spirit, and yet, I'm not speaking of an evil spirit. That's not what it is. It is the spirit or nature of the individual. That spirit or nature can be holy as it's intended to be, or it can be unholy.

That's what Paul was talking about here when he said: *"Neither yield you your members as instruments of unrighteousness unto sin: but yield yourselves unto God, as those who are alive from the dead, and your members as instruments of righteousness unto God"* (Rom. 6:13).

The Holy Spirit through Paul is telling us here that the physical members of our body are neutral. It means they are not holy or unholy. They are whatever we make them. The real you is the *inward man,* actually, the soul and the spirit. You are a living soul, and you have a spirit. And yet, all you really need to know as it regards the sin nature is that your faith must be in Christ and what Christ did for you at the Cross.

SPIRITUAL AUTHORITY

If the believer's faith is in anything except the Cross of Christ, in the eyes of God, that believer is functioning in a state of spiritual adultery (Rom. 7:1-4). The sad thing is, most believers have never even heard of spiritual adultery, much less understand what it actually is.

When we were born again, in effect, we married the Lord Jesus Christ (II Cor. 11:1-4). Being married to Him, He is to meet our every need, which He alone can do. He does so by the means of the Cross, which then gives the Holy Spirit, as stated, liberty to work.

THE ADMONITION

As is obvious, Hezekiah had a burden for the northern kingdom of Israel, as well as his own country of Judah. No doubt, the Holy Spirit guided him in the information imparted to his northern neighbor. He said to them, *"You children of Israel, turn again unto the Lord God of Abraham, Isaac, and Israel, and He will return to the remnant of you, who are escaped out of the hand of the kings of Assyria."*

He admonished them to be *"not stiffnecked, as your fathers were, but yield yourselves unto the Lord, and enter into His sanctuary."* Then the promise was given, *"For the Lord your God is gracious and merciful, and will not turn away His face from you, if you return unto Him."*

GRACE AND MERCY

How right Hezekiah was. If anyone shows any inclination at all toward the Lord with any degree of repentance, or if there is anyone with a broken and contrite spirit, even to a small degree, the Lord will always be *"gracious and merciful"* and will not turn away His face from you. What a beautiful promise!

As the Holy Spirit spoke through Hezekiah, the great promise, as well, was given that if those in the northern kingdom would serve God, Israel, which had been taken over by the Assyrians, would once again become a viable nation. That never happened!

Some years later, because of her sin and shame, the southern kingdom of Judah fell to the Babylonians. They remained some 70 years in captivity, with a remnant of them coming back, from which the entirety of the nation was once again established. At any rate, Hezekiah tried.

THE MOCKERY OF THE NORTHERN KINGDOM

So the posts passed from city to city through the country of Ephraim and Manasseh even unto Zebulun: but they laughed them to scorn, and mocked them. Nevertheless divers of Asher and Manasseh and of Zebulun humbled themselves, and came to Jerusalem. Also in Judah the hand of God was to give them one heart to do the commandment of the king and of the princes, by the word of the Lord. And there assembled at Jerusalem much people to keep the Feast of Unleavened Bread in the second month, a very great congregation. And they arose and took away the altars that were in Jerusalem, and all the altars for incense took they away, and cast them into the brook Kidron (II Chron. 30:10-14).

THE FEASTS

The last two phrases of verse 10 give a significant description of the exact moral state in which Israel's tribes were now to be found. Sadly, far too many in the modern church meet the Message of the Cross with laughter, scorn, and mockery.

While many, in fact, will laugh and mock, still, many will accept and receive. It is to the latter we look! As it speaks of the *"Feast of Unleavened Bread"* in verse 13, in actuality, three feasts were to be conducted at this time: *"Passover, Unleavened Bread, and Firstfruits."* That took seven days:

- Passover commenced on the first day. It signified Calvary.

- Unleavened Bread was spread over the entire seven days. It signified the perfect life and perfect body of Christ, which would be offered in sacrifice on the Cross of Calvary.

- Firstfruits took place the last day. It typified the resurrection of Christ.

THE MOCKING AND THE LAUGHING

Concerning this Passover, this great feast ordained by Hezekiah was one of the 10 great Passovers of the Bible.

George Williams said:

Certain facts connected with its observance prove that the Pentateuch was read, loved, and obeyed by Hezekiah. He invited all Israel; he kept the Feast in the second month instead of the first [Num. 9]; he ordained that it should be observed 'as it is written' [Lev. 23]; he declared that their miseries were those predicted in Deuteronomy; that God would have compassion upon them if they turned unto Him, as promised in Deuteronomy; that all was to be regulated by the Word of the Lord, i.e., by the Bible; that the priests should officiate according to the law of Moses; he pointed out to the people that many of them were not ceremonially clean according to the Scriptures; learning that a great multitude ate the passover 'otherwise than it was written', he prayed that they might be pardoned, thus showing his reverence for the Bible, and his fear of disobeying it [Lev. 15:31]; he believed the threatened plague to be a reality; he kept the Feast of Unleavened Bread seven days because so the Book of God ordained; and, in a word, in the observance of the Feast, he confined himself within the leaves of the Bible.

Irrespective of this great move of God in Judah, still, many of the remnant who were left in the northern kingdom of what once had been Israel had no heart for God. The Scripture says, when invited to the Passover, they mocked the messengers and laughed them to scorn.

THE HEART OF MAN

Why is it that there is a terrible animosity in the hearts of men as it regards the Lord? The animosity is not found as it regards any other religion, no matter how base or how vile the other religion might be. Irrespective that untold millions of lives have been gloriously and wondrously changed by the power of God, still, Jesus Christ is lampooned in so many circles or simply ignored.

Why?

As far as I know, there is no profanity in any language of the world that lambasts, mocks, and profanes the religion of the land. It is only Christianity toward which such vituperation is enjoined.

The following constitutes some of the reasons for the vituperation against the Lord:

- The God of Israel given to us in the Bible is, in fact, the only true God. All else is fake; consequently, Satan levels his attack against Jehovah.

- It all stems from the fall in the garden of Eden. From that moment, there has been an animosity in the heart of man against God. If man does not blaspheme God outright, at the very least, he tries to ignore Him.

• As it regards Jehovah, the name, "the Lord Jesus Christ," is hated by the powers of darkness and those who follow Satan (which constitutes the majority) as nothing else. Why? Jesus Christ is the only way to God (Jn. 14:6), which thwarts Satan's efforts at directing mankind to another way.

To sum up, the animosity is in the heart of man against the Lord simply because the Lord of the Bible is the Lord, and despite all the claims, there is no other. To be sure, Satan will not lampoon and lambaste that which he has originated, and I speak of all the false religions and false gods.

As well, all those who do not know the Lord are children of Satan and, thereby, have an inbred hatred against Christ.

THE ACCEPTANCE OF THE LORD

Despite those who laughed and mocked, the Scripture says, *"Nevertheless divers of Asher and Manasseh and of Zebulun humbled themselves, and came to Jerusalem."*

That's the way it always has been. Many, if not most, laugh and mock, but some will accept, and all who do accept the Lord will prove to be a light in the darkness.

Why do some accept and some reject? Why will some few have a heart toward God if given the opportunity, while others given the same opportunity will reject? Why did Jacob love the Lord and Esau rebel against the Lord, considering they were brothers, even twins?

No one has the answers to those questions.

One thing we do know: God does not force the issue. He will deal with man, speak to man, and move upon man, but He will not force man to do anything. Man is a free moral agent. He has the capacity to say yes or to say no, at least as it regards the acceptance or rejection of the Lord Jesus Christ.

THE WILL OF MAN

While Satan most definitely can override the will of man, which he does constantly, there remains the capacity in the heart of all men to say yes to Jesus Christ.

In other words, the Lord safeguards that capacity in every respect.

At this moment, there are millions in the world who try to say no to alcohol, drugs, or other evils but are unable to do so because the powers of darkness are stronger than their wills. Still, those same individuals, if they so desire, can say yes to Jesus Christ, which then gives Him an opportunity to set them free from the terrible vices that darken their lives.

If my memory is correct, John Bunyan, who wrote *Pilgrim's Progress,* which influenced Christianity greatly, was a drunk before he gave his heart to Christ. He was not only a drunk but what is labeled as a mean drunk, a wife beater, the kind of individual that is despicable to say the least.

THE POWER OF THE HOLY SPIRIT

Bunyan realized that his life was being totally wrecked, and besides that, he was destroying his wife and children. After a particular bout of drunkenness, it is said that he walked out into a field, fell down on his knees, and began to pray. To be sure, his praying was very weak to say the least. In fact, he did not know how to pray, but under conviction because of the prayers of his wife, all he knew to do was to say the following:

Gentle Jesus, meek and mild,
Please have pity on a little child,
Please suffer my simplicity,
And allow me to come to Thee.

That was his prayer, actually, merely a little childhood prayer, but God heard it, and at that moment, Jesus Christ changed the heart and life of John Bunyan.

If any man, woman, boy, or girl shows the slightest inclination toward the Lord, mercy will always be forthcoming, and grace will always be freely given. The Scripture plainly says to us, *"Whosoever shall call upon the name of the Lord shall be saved"* (Rom. 10:13).

THE DESTRUCTION OF THE HEATHEN ALTARS

Whenever the word of the Lord begins to be practiced, begins to take effect, and begins to be propagated among the people, the heathen altars have to go.

What would constitute a heathen altar at this present time, and we speak of modern times?

The answer is simple: Any worship and any homage that is paid to anything other than Jesus Christ and Him crucified would be constituted in the mind of God as a heathen altar. Paul said, *"For whatsoever is not of faith is sin"* (Rom. 14:23).

The type of faith addressed here is faith in Jesus Christ and Him crucified; any other type of faith in believers is sin.

The great apostle also said, and I quote from The Expositor's Study Bible:

"Examine yourselves, whether you be in the faith (the words, 'the faith,' refer to "Christ and Him crucified," with the Cross ever being the object of our faith); *prove your own selves.* (Make certain your faith is actually in the Cross and not other things.) *Know you not your own selves, how that Jesus Christ is in you* (which He can only be by our faith expressed in His sacrifice), *except you be reprobates?* (Rejected)" (II Cor. 13:5).

Satan cannot stop the gospel as the great work of Calvary is already a historic fact. So, he seeks to pervert the gospel, and he has been very successful at doing that.

THE NEW COVENANT

Jesus Christ is the new covenant. By that I mean He doesn't merely have the new covenant, or is not merely the arbiter of the new covenant, but, in fact, is the new covenant. As God is love, which means that Jesus is love, as well, and because He is God, likewise, the Lord Jesus Christ is the new covenant.

The meaning of the new covenant is the Cross of Christ exactly as it was given to the apostle Paul, and he gave to us in his 14 epistles.

As previously stated, Jesus Christ is the source of everything we receive from God, while the Cross is the means by which these things are given to us, all superintended by the Holy Spirit (Rom. 6:1-14; 8:1-11; I Cor. 1:17-18, 21, 23; 2:2; Gal. 5; 6:14; Eph. 2:13-18; Col. 2:10-15).

It is all in Christ and what He did at the Cross. Unfortunately, the Evil One has been very successful at making things other than the Cross of Christ the object of one's faith. Always remember the following: Jesus Christ and what He did for us at the Cross is to always be the object of our faith. If our faith is in anything else, and I mean anything else—no matter how scriptural the other thing might be in its own right—such constitutes sin.

So, unfortunately, the heathen altars continue to abound at the present time. God help us that the church comes back to the Cross. If it does, the part of the modern church that does come back to the Cross will, without a doubt, eradicate the heathen altars. It had to be done in the days of Hezekiah, and it must be done presently.

THE LORD HEALED THE PEOPLE

Then they killed the passover on the fourteenth day of the second month: and the priests and the Levites were ashamed, and sanctified themselves, and brought in the burnt offerings into the house of the LORD. And they stood in their place after their manner, according to the law of Moses the man of God: the priests sprinkled the blood, which they received of the hand of the Levites. For there were many in the congregation who were not sanctified: therefore the Levites had the charge of the killing of the passovers for everyone who was not clean, to sanctify them unto the LORD. For a multitude of the people, even many of Ephraim, and Manasseh, Issachar, and Zebulun, had not cleansed themselves, yet did they eat the passover otherwise than it was written. But Hezekiah prayed for them, saying, The good LORD pardon everyone that prepares his heart to seek God, the LORD God of his fathers, though he be not cleansed according to the purification of the sanctuary. And the LORD hearkened to Hezekiah, and healed the people (II Chron. 30:15-20).

Verse 15 speaks of repentance on the part of the priests and the Levites. Judgment must begin at the house of God (I Pet. 4:17).

Verse 17 affirms that the original direction of Moses was that the person who brought the victim was to kill it, but, in this case, the Levites mostly officiated.

The reason all of this was so serious is simply because it all pointed to Christ and what He would do to redeem humanity, which all led to the Cross. There is no healing other than Calvary. All other cisterns are broken and *"can hold no water"* (Jer. 2:13).

THE KILLING OF THE PASSOVER

The manner and the way in which this was to be carried out was according to the following: The individual would bring the lamb to the priest. The man bringing the lamb would lay both hands on the head of the animal and then confess his sins, whatever they may have been. This constituted a transference of his sin to the innocent victim, which was a type of Christ carrying the penalty of our sins upon Himself on the Cross. When this was accomplished, the individual was to take a sharp knife and cut the jugular vein of the animal, with the hot blood then pouring into a basin, which was held by the priest. This typified our Lord shedding His blood on Calvary's Cross.

The individual bringing the lamb had to kill the animal because he was the one who had sinned and, therefore, must perform the deed. It was our sins that nailed Christ to the Cross and certainly not sins that He had committed.

When the artists paint the picture of Jesus hanging on the Cross, and do so in all of its horror, at least as far as one can do, we must look at that portrayal, and we must say, "My sins did that."

THE SIN OFFERING

The type of offering presented at the Passover was a sin offering. This particular offering portrayed the sins of the individual being transferred to Christ, as should be obvious. Conversely, the whole burnt offering constituted the very opposite. It symbolized the perfection of Christ being given to the sinner. So, we have in these two offerings the sins of the sinner being given to Christ and the perfection of Christ being given to the sinner. All of this was a type of Calvary.

Due to ignorance and the Passover being hastily instituted, there were many Israelites who were not properly sanctified. So, they could not kill the animal, with that being left up to the priests, who carried out the task.

THE SIGNIFICANCE OF THE PASSOVER

As is obvious, the Passover represented Christ and what He would do at the Cross. Hezekiah knew that many of the people had eaten unworthily, so the Scripture says that *"Hezekiah prayed for them, saying, The good LORD pardon every one who prepares his heart to seek God, the LORD God of his fathers, though he be not cleansed according to the purification of the sanctuary."*

Then the Scripture says, *"And the LORD hearkened to Hezekiah, and healed the people."* In a sense, the Lord's Supper is an outgrowth of the Passover. The Passover looked forward to something that was to come, namely, the Lord Jesus Christ and what He would do at the Cross. The Lord's Supper looks backward to a work already finished, hence, the admonition, *"This do in remembrance of Me"* (I Cor. 11:24).

THE LORD'S SUPPER

Concerning this, Paul said, and I quote from The Expositor's Study Bible:

> *For as often as you eat this bread, and drink this cup* (symbolic gestures), *you do show the Lord's death till He come.* (This is

meant to proclaim not only the Atoning Sacrifice necessary for our Salvation but, as well, as an ongoing cause of our continued victory in life.) *Wherefore whosoever shall eat this bread, and drink this cup of the Lord, unworthily* (tells us emphatically that this can be done and is done constantly, I'm afraid), *shall be guilty of the body and blood of the Lord* (in danger of judgment, subject to judgment). *But let a man examine himself* (examine his faith as to what is its real object), *and so let him eat of* that *bread, and drink of that cup* (after careful examination). *For he who eats and drinks unworthily, eats and drinks damnation to himself* (does not necessarily mean the loss of one's soul, but rather temporal penalties, which can become much more serious), *not discerning the Lord's Body*. (Not properly discerning the Cross refers to a lack of understanding regarding the Cross. All of this tells us that every single thing we have from the Lord comes to us exclusively by means of the Cross of Christ. If we do not understand that, we are not properly 'discerning the Lord's Body.')

ONE'S LIFE CUT SHORT

For this cause (not properly discerning the Lord's body) *many* (a considerable number) *are weak and sickly among you* (the cause of much sickness among Christians), *and many sleep.* (This means that many Christians die prematurely. They don't lose their souls, but they do cut their lives short. This shows us, I seriously think, how important properly understanding the Cross is.) *For if we would judge ourselves* (we should examine ourselves constantly, as to whether our faith is properly placed in the Cross of Christ), *we should not be judged* (with sickness, and even premature death). *But when we are judged* (by the Lord because we refuse to judge ourselves), *we are chastened of the Lord* (Divine discipline), *that we should not be condemned with the world* (lose our soul) (I Cor. 11:26-32).

FAITH

The Lord does not require sinless perfection in order for one to partake of that which is referred to as *"the Lord's Supper."* However, He most definitely has clearly given instructions here in Scripture that our faith be exclusively in Christ and what Christ has done for us at the Cross. Unfortunately, at this present time, the faith of far too many Christians is placed in something other than Christ and Him crucified. As a result, and exactly as the Word of God proclaims, if the truth be known, many Christians are physically ill because of not properly discerning the Lord's body, and then, some even die prematurely. While the cause of death may be listed in any capacity, the truth is, it is because of this very thing that we have here addressed. Their faith is in something other than Christ and Him crucified. Unfortunately, their faith is in their church, their religious denomination, their good works, the money they have given, religious activity, etc.

Please understand, as I think by now should be obvious, this is serious business. We must treat it accordingly!

PRAISING THE LORD

"And the children of Israel who were present at Jerusalem kept the feast of unleavened bread seven days with great gladness: and the Levites and the priests praised the LORD *day by day, singing with loud instruments unto the* LORD. *And Hezekiah spoke comfortably unto all the Levites who taught the good knowledge of the* LORD: *and they did eat throughout the feast seven days, offering peace offerings, and making confession to the* LORD *God of their fathers"* (II Chron. 30:21-22).

Once again, even as we see in verse 21, worship in the realm of music and singing always accompanies the Cross and our faith in that finished work.

The peace offering was the only offering eaten in part by the offerer. Almost always, peace offerings were offered with the sin offering, the whole burnt offering, and the trespass offering. It signified that God had accepted the offering and that peace, which had been interrupted, was now restored between God and man.

As well, most of the time, a meat offering (thank offering) was offered also. This is the only one of the five offerings that contained no flesh. It was always made up of flour, cereal, etc. It was pure and simple a thanksgiving offering.

THE PEACE OFFERING

As stated, peace offerings almost always accompanied the sin, the trespass, and whole burnt offerings. In fact, it was the only offering of which both the priests and the person bringing the offering partook.

The idea was, now that the sin, trespass, or whole burnt offering had been offered up to the Lord, which meant that the sin had been expiated, it was now a time for rejoicing. In fact, the individual bringing the offering could take the part given to him, call in his friends and neighbors if he so desired, and have a feast. It was to be a time of rejoicing before the Lord, and for all the obvious reasons. As stated, due to the sacrifice offered, peace had now been restored, hence, the peace offering. That's the reason the Scripture says, "... *the feast of unleavened bread seven days with great gladness: and the Levites and the priests praised the* LORD *day by day, singing with loud instruments unto the* LORD."

GREAT JOY IN JERUSALEM

And the whole assembly took counsel to keep other seven days: and they kept other seven days with gladness. For Hezekiah king of Judah did give to the congregation a thousand bullocks and seven thousand sheep; and the princes gave to the congregation a thousand bullocks and ten thousand sheep: and a great number of priests sanctified themselves. And all the congregation of Judah, with the priests and the Levites, and all the congregation that came out of Israel, and the strangers who came out of the land of Israel, and who dwelt in Judah, rejoiced. So there was great joy in Jerusalem: for since the time of Solomon the son of David king of Israel there was not the like in Jerusalem. Then the priests the Levites arose and blessed the people: and their voice was heard, and their prayer came up to His holy dwelling place, even unto heaven (II Chron. 30:23-27).

The conduits carrying the blood from these many sacrifices from the temple mount would have caused the brook Kidron, which ran between the temple mount and Mount Olivet, to run red with blood.

This is obnoxious and repulsive to the unspiritual eye, but to those who know their God, Calvary is the greatest sight this side of heaven, for it was there that man was liberated and set free (Col. 2:10-15). Calvary alone brings great joy; nothing else will.

The only prayer that God will hear is that which is anchored in Calvary's Cross. In fact, as human beings, no matter what good we may think we do, such has no standing with God. Our standing with Him pertains exclusively to the Lord Jesus Christ, what He did at Calvary, and our faith in that finished work.

THE SACRIFICES

As is here glaringly obvious, the blessing, prosperity, and greatness of Judah all depended upon the shed blood of the Lamb, of which all the sacrifices were a type. It is no different presently. The blessings of the modern church, and especially each individual, are all predicated on Calvary, i.e., what Jesus there did. However, let it ever be understood that the one sacrifice of Himself given at Calvary's Cross was greater, far greater, than all of the hundreds of thousands, and even millions, of animal sacrifices that had been offered up, even from the beginning of time. That's the reason that the entirety of the new covenant is anchored in the Lord Jesus Christ and what He did at the Cross. In other words, the new covenant is the

Lord Jesus Christ. It has no altars, at least the kind on which sacrifices are made, no temples, no rituals, and no ceremonies other than water baptism, which is a one-time affair, and the Lord's Supper, which should be taken at given times. All of this is symbolic of the Cross of Christ and, in fact, is meant to bring the believer back to the Cross.

THE CROSS

Concerning all of this which Hezekiah did, the Scripture says it was:

- With gladness

- Rejoicing

- Great joy

I think it should be obvious by now that everything, as it relates to the Lord, is tied to the Cross.

As stated, no matter how good we might think we are, and no matter how many good works we might carry out, within ourselves, we have no standing with the Lord whatsoever. Any standing that we have is ours simply because of the Lord Jesus Christ, what He has done for us at the Cross, and our faith in that finished work. We must never forget that. That must be the core, the central focus of our life and living for God. It is the Cross! The Cross!

Just as I am, without one plea,
But that Your blood was shed for me,
And that You bid me come to Thee,
O Lamb of God, I come!

Just as I am and waiting not
To rid my soul of one dark blot;
To Thee whose blood can cleanse each spot,
O Lamb of God I come!

Just as I am though tossed about,
With many a conflict, many a doubt;
Fightings within and fears without,
O Lamb of God I come!

Just as I am, poor, wretched, blind;
Sight, riches, healing of the mind;
Yea all I need in Thee to find,
O Lamb of God I come!

Just as I am, You will receive,
Will welcome, pardon, cleanse, and relieve;
Because Your promise I believe,
O Lamb of God I come!

Just as I am Your love unknown,
Has broken every barrier down;
Now to be Thine yea Thine alone,
O Lamb of God I come!

Just as I am, of that great love,
The breadth, length, depth,
The height to prove,
Here for a season, then above,
O Lamb of God I come.

HEZEKIAH

CHAPTER 3

HE DID IT WITH ALL HIS
HEART, AND PROSPERED

HE DID IT WITH ALL HIS HEART, AND PROSPERED

"*Now when all this was finished, all Israel that were present went out to the cities of Judah, and broke the images in pieces, and cut down the groves, and threw down the high places and the altars out of all Judah and Benjamin, in Ephraim also and Manasseh, until they had utterly destroyed them all. Then all the children of Israel returned, every man to his possession, into their own cities*" (II Chron. 31:1).

THE REVIVAL

A revival, that is, if it's scriptural, necessitates several things. Before there could be revival, Judah had to come back to the Cross, typified by the sacrifices. Likewise, before there can be revival in the church or even in the heart and life of the individual, the church or the individual must come back to the Cross as well. Everything begins at the Cross. Any effort made without taking the Cross into account is a wasted effort.

WHY IS THE CROSS THAT NECESSARY?

The Cross of Christ is where all sin was atoned and where Satan and all of his demon spirits and fallen angels were defeated, thereby, making it possible for the grace of God to be extended to believing man in an unprecedented manner (Col. 2:10-15). The Cross of Christ tells man what he is, tells man who and what God is, and puts everything in proper perspective. In fact, every truth of the Bible is built squarely on the Cross, and if our interpretation is false, that means the Cross is interpreted wrongly or ignored altogether (I Pet. 1:18-20).

As we stated previously, irrespective of how good man may think he is, or how good others may think he is, within himself, man has absolutely no standing with God whatsoever. In other words, if we try to come to the Lord on our own merit, the door will be closed. Man has access to God, access to His throne, and access to all that God is simply by and through the Cross of Christ and no other way. In other words, when we come in prayer to the throne, we must come in the name of Jesus, which was all made possible by the Cross (Jn. 16:23). This is a great truth that we must ever understand (Eph. 2:13-18).

REDEMPTION

While man may admit that certain people of the human race may need the Cross, it is hard for those who consider themselves to be moral to admit their need for Christ and the Cross. However, it is like one leper claiming that he's better than another leper because he has only 142 leprous spots, while the other leper has 145 leprous spots. The moral is, all of mankind is constituted as sinful lepers, meaning that man desperately needs a redeemer, and that redeemer is the Lord Jesus Christ and, in fact, can only be the Lord Jesus Christ. There is no other! As well, Christ is the Redeemer by and through what He did at the Cross. The Cross is ever the catalyst for all things pertaining to the Lord and man.

DOES THE MODERN CHURCH BELIEVE
THAT THE CROSS IS THE CATALYST?

In a word, no!

Incidentally, one of the meanings of the word *catalyst* is "that which brings about change," which is the way it is used here.

A great part of the church places no confidence at all in the Cross of Christ. Another part of the church claims to believe the Cross but projects a claim in name only. In other words, the Cross of Christ in those circles is very seldom mentioned. If it is mentioned, it is mentioned only in the capacity of the salvation process. Thank the Lord for that; however, that is only a part of what the Lord gave to the apostle Paul as it regarded the meaning of the new covenant, which is the meaning of the Cross. Only a small part of the modern church actually believes and understands that the Cross of Christ is the center of all things as it relates to the Lord and His Word.

CAIN AND ABEL

The stage is set in Chapter 4 of Genesis, as it regards that which God demands and man's reaction to that demand.

The Lord conveyed to the first family that even though they were fallen, they could have forgiveness of sins and fellowship with Him through the sacrifice of an innocent victim, namely a lamb. That lamb would typify Christ who was to come, i.e., the seed of the woman. However, it would be only by the slain lamb that such could be attained.

It seems that Cain was the first of the two brothers to offer up a sacrifice. The Scripture says of this man, *"That Cain brought of the fruit of the ground an offering unto the Lord."* The Scripture also says, *"And Abel, he also brought of the firstlings of his flock and of the fat thereof."* The words, *"He also brought,"* places Abel as second to Cain.

However, then the Scripture tells us, *"And the Lord had respect unto Abel and to his offering: But unto Cain and to his offering He had not respect"* (Gen. 4:3-5).

A LAMB—AN INNOCENT VICTIM

It seems that Cain did not deny the need for an offering, but that he desired to offer up that which he had selected and not that which God had demanded.

These offerings, which were on the first page of human history, set the stage for all that would follow thereafter. The Lord accepted the offering of Abel because it was what He demanded, which was a lamb, an innocent victim that would be typical of the coming Redeemer, the Lord Jesus Christ.

As well, it addressed man in need of a redeemer, and that redeemer could only be Christ. The Lord rejected the offering of Cain because it was the *"fruit of the ground"* and did not address the problem, which was sin. Sin could only be addressed by an innocent victim, i.e., a lamb.

THE OFFERING WAS THE CATALYST

The Lord didn't even really look at the ones bringing the offering because it was obvious what they were. Both Cain and Abel were born outside of Eden, meaning they were born in original sin, and meaning they were both lost. He rather looked at the offering. If the offering met His specifications, then the offerer was accepted also. If the offering was rejected, likewise, the offerer was rejected. This means that Abel was accepted, while Cain was rejected.

It has not changed from then until now. The Lord looks at our faith, and more particularly, the object of our faith. The object must be the Cross of Christ, that is, if it is to be accepted. If our faith is in the proper object, then we are automatically accepted as well. If it's not in the proper object, namely the Cross of Christ, then the individual is instantly rejected.

THE FIRST MURDER

The first murder among the human family was because of religion.

Cain was angry because God had accepted the offering of Abel, his brother, and had rejected his, so he murdered his brother.

George Williams said concerning this, "Cain's religion was too refined to kill a lamb but not too cultured to murder his brother. God's way of salvation fills the heart with love; man's way of salvation enflames it with hatred. 'Religion' has ever been the greatest cause of bloodshed."

Those who reject the Cross of Christ are not content to go their own way but feel they must, as Cain, eliminate those who believe in the one sacrifice accepted by the Lord. As stated, it hasn't changed from then until now. The Cross was an offense to Cain, and it is an offense to millions at present.

HOW IS THE CROSS OF CHRIST AN OFFENSE?

Paul said, *"And I, brethren, if I yet preach circumcision, why do I yet suffer persecution?* (any message other than the Cross draws little opposition) *then is the offence of the Cross ceased.* (The Cross offends the world and most of the church. So, if the preacher ceases to preach the Cross as the only way of salvation and victory, then opposition and persecution will cease, but so will salvation and victory)*"* (Gal. 5:11) (The Expositor's Study Bible).

The Cross of Christ is an offense simply because it lays waste all of man's efforts to save himself or to sanctify himself. In other words, it shows what man really is, a poor, disconsolate, stumbling, and halting creature, who, because of the fall, cannot even keep the slightest commandment given by the Lord.

But man does not like to admit that. He—especially religious man—likes to think that whatever is necessary as it regards spiritual things, he can do. As a believer, he is loath to admit that he cannot effect his own sanctification, and that he cannot overcome the efforts by the Evil One to steal, kill, and destroy.

When the preacher stands up, even as Paul, and lays waste all of man's efforts, that offends because it lays waste the flesh. In other words, when a preacher states that the only way to salvation and the only way to victory is by and through the Lord Jesus Christ and what He did at the Cross and our faith in that finished work, this offends religious man. However, faith in that finished work of the Cross is what enables the Holy Spirit to effect His great work within our lives.

WHAT IS THE FLESH?

The flesh can actually be described in two ways. They are:

1. Man's personal ability, personal strength, education, motivation, knowledge, wisdom, efforts, talents, intellectualism, etc. While these things may or may not be wrong in their own right, the idea is, what we need to be in Christ and, in fact, what we must be in Christ cannot be effected by our own personal efforts. Due to the fall, man has been rendered incapable (Rom. 8:10).

2. The flesh can also pertain to ungodly desires and passions and, thereby, is unholy. The flesh will always

gravitate toward that, hence, the reason the Scripture says, *"So then they who are in the flesh cannot please God"* (Rom. 8:8). That's the reason Paul also said, *"For they who are after the flesh do mind the things of the flesh; but they who are after the Spirit the things of the Spirit"* (Rom. 8:5). That's the reason we are emphatically told to *"walk not after the flesh"* (Rom. 8:1).

WHAT IS WALKING AFTER THE FLESH?

Of course, we are speaking of believers. All unbelievers walk exclusively after the flesh because that's the only way they can function. The Spirit of God does not dwell in them, as is obvious, so the flesh is their only alternative, hence, the reason for all sin, man's inhumanity to man, ungodliness, crime, etc.

Walking after the flesh constitutes the believer placing his or her faith in anything, irrespective as to what it might be, other than Christ and the Cross (Rom. 6:1-14; 8:1-11; I Cor. 1:17-18, 21, 23; 2:2; Col. 2:10-15).

Many believers think that because their faith is in something religious, it is satisfactory with the Lord. It isn't! In fact, walking after the Spirit, which, of course, refers to the Holy Spirit, constitutes the believer placing his or her faith exclusively in Christ and the Cross (Rom. 8:2).

Many Christians think that the doing of spiritual things— such as witnessing to people about the Lord, giving money to the work of God, fasting, etc.—constitutes walking after the Spirit. While those things are certainly necessary and are a part of Christian disciplines, still, that's not walking after the Spirit. As stated, walking after the Spirit refers to the believer placing his or her faith exclusively in Christ and what Christ has done for us at the Cross (Rom. 8:1-11).

WHAT IS IT THAT THE SPIRIT DOES WHICH WE ARE SUPPOSED TO EMULATE?

The Holy Spirit, without whom we can do nothing, works exclusively within the framework of the finished work of Christ, i.e., the Cross (Rom. 8:2).

Knowing and understanding how the Holy Spirit works is half the battle, so to speak. Unfortunately, so many in the church presently take the Holy Spirit for granted, and that results in great difficulties.

Before the Cross, the Holy Spirit could not dwell in the hearts and lives of believers. He could dwell in certain ones, such as prophets or some few kings, for a short period of time, enabling them to carry out what He had called them to do, but permanently, no, He could not! He was *with* them, but He could not reside *in* them (Jn. 14:16-17).

But the Cross changed all of that. Now, the moment the believing sinner accepts Christ, the Holy Spirit comes in to abide forever (Jn. 14:16). Please understand that there is a vast difference in the Holy Spirit being with us than the Holy Spirit being in us. No doubt, the Holy Spirit being with an individual was wonderful, but his being in us is the greatest thing of all.

As well, when believers died before the Cross, they could not go to heaven. Why?

It was because the blood of bulls and goats could not take away sins (Heb. 10:4). Due to the fact that animal blood was insufficient, the sin debt remained, which meant that they could not enter heaven. However, their souls and their spirits were taken to paradise where they were comforted, but they were there awaiting the Cross. The moment the Cross was a fact, Jesus delivered all of those people out of paradise, making them His captives and taking them to heaven. Since the Cross, when a believer passes away, his soul and his spirit instantly go to heaven to be with the Lord Jesus Christ.

So, all of this means that the Holy Spirit works exclusively in the Cross. It's the Cross of Christ that gave Him and gives Him the legal means to do all that He does. That's the reason that Paul wrote:

"For the law of the Spirit of life (Holy Spirit) *in Christ Jesus has made me free from the law of sin and death"* (Rom. 8:2).

The words *"in Christ Jesus,"* or any one of its derivatives, such as "in Him," etc., refer to the Holy Spirit working exclusively within the parameters of the Cross of Christ. The Holy Spirit doesn't demand much of us, but He most definitely does demand that our faith be exclusively in Christ and the Cross (Rom. 6:1-14; 8:1-11; Eph. 2:13-18; Gal., Chpt. 5; 6:14; Col. 2:10-15).

If the Holy Spirit works exclusively by and through the Cross, which He most definitely does, this means that our faith must ever be in Christ and the Cross. If our faith is in anything other than Christ and the Cross, in essence, we are living in a state of spiritual adultery.

WHAT IS SPIRITUAL ADULTERY?

Spiritual adultery is the believer, who is married to Christ, being unfaithful to Christ. How does the believer be unfaithful to Christ? (II Cor. 11:1-4).

Being unfaithful to Christ and, thereby, living in a state of spiritual adultery means that the believer is unfaithful to Christ, which means that he places his faith in something else other than Christ and the Cross. In fact, at one time or the other, every single believer who has ever lived has tried to function in the realm of spiritual adultery. In fact, this is what the entirety of Chapter 7 of Romans is all about. It is a proclamation of the experience of the apostle Paul after he was saved, Spirit-filled, and preaching the gospel. At that particular time, he did not know God's prescribed order of victory, which is the Cross of Christ, and in his defense, no one else did either. In fact, it was to the apostle Paul that this great revelation was given (Gal. 1:12).

THE SEVENTH CHAPTER OF ROMANS

In Chapter 7 of Romans, the apostle gives us the account of his life and experience after he was saved on the road to Damascus. How long he was in this state of spiritual failure, we are not told; however, it must have been at least a year or two. Despite all of his efforts otherwise, he found he could not successfully live for the Lord, and if the apostle Paul couldn't successfully live for the Lord in this capacity, in other words, keep the commandments of the Lord, neither can you nor I.

The Holy Spirit works entirely, as stated, within the framework of the finished work of Christ, and in view of this, we are expected to have our faith anchored squarely in the Cross of Christ. In other words, the Cross of Christ is to ever be the object of our faith because that's where the victory was won by Christ (Col. 2:14-15). When the believer anchors his faith exclusively in the Cross of Christ and doesn't allow it to be moved elsewhere, this means that such a believer is being faithful to Christ. When the believer anchors his faith exclusively in the Cross of Christ and doesn't allow it to be moved elsewhere, the Holy Spirit will then work mightily within his heart and life, developing His fruit, which He alone can do.

LET US SAY IT AGAIN ...

Spiritual adultery constitutes the believer placing his faith in something other than the Cross of Christ. As also stated, every believer is married to Christ (Rom. 7:4; II Cor. 11:1-4). As such, and as should be obvious, Christ is to meet our every need, which, in fact, He alone can do. However, when we place our faith in something other than Christ and what He has done at the Cross, this constitutes spiritual adultery. In effect, we are being unfaithful to Christ, which, as you can imagine, greatly hinders the Holy Spirit. Thank God that the Spirit does not leave us in those times, because He loves us. Instead, He does everything He can do to help us, but the truth is, we greatly limit Him, as should be obvious, whenever our faith is misplaced.

FAITH

The believer must understand that every single thing we do and the way we live for the Lord is all constituted by faith. However, it must also be understood that the object of our faith must always be Christ and the Cross. This is where the problem comes in. We have faith, but it's misplaced faith. It's faith in the wrong object, which the Holy Spirit can never honor. Jesus said that when the Holy Spirit comes, and He most definitely has already come, *"He shall glorify Me* (will portray Christ and what Christ did at the Cross for lost humanity): *for He shall receive of Mine* (the benefits of the Cross), *and shall show it unto you* (which He did when He gave these great truths to the Apostle Paul, and Paul gave them to us in his 14 epistles)" (Jn. 16:14) (The Expositor's Study Bible).

Every victory was won at the Cross, and as previously stated, Satan and all of his cohorts of darkness were defeated at the Cross. So, that's where the believer must anchor his faith. That is the Word of God (Eph. 2:13-18; Col. 2:14-15; Gal., Chpt. 5; 6:14).

THE LAW OF THE LORD

And Hezekiah appointed the courses of the priests and the Levites after their courses, every man according to his service, the priests and the Levites for burnt offerings and for peace offerings, to minister, and to give thanks, and to praise in the gates of the tents of the LORD. He appointed also the king's portion of his substance for the burnt offerings, to wit, for the morning and evening burnt offerings, and the burnt offerings for the Sabbaths, and for the new moons, and for the set feasts, as it is written in the law of the LORD. Moreover he commanded the people who dwelt in Jerusalem to give the portion of the priests and the Levites, that they might be encouraged in the law of the LORD. And as soon as the commandment came abroad, the children of Israel brought in abundance the firstfruits of corn, wine, and oil, and honey, and of all the increase of the field; and the tithe of all things brought they in abundantly. And concerning the children of Israel and Judah, who dwelt in the cities of Judah, they also brought in the tithe of oxen and sheep, and the tithe of the holy things which were consecrated unto the LORD their God, and laid them by heaps. In the third month they began to lay the foundation of the heaps, and finished them in the seventh month. And when Hezekiah and the princes came and saw the heaps, they blessed the LORD, and His people Israel. Then Hezekiah questioned with the priests and the Levites concerning the heaps (II Chron. 31:2-9).

THE BIBLE

Offering sacrifices and giving thanks to the Lord were thought of as so much foolishness by King Ahaz, the father of Hezekiah. Likewise, the carnal mind rejects the Word of the Lord, but the spiritual mind understands its value. If we ignore the Bible, we lose our love for God. If we love the Bible, we will love God. Hezekiah loved the Bible, so he would obey the Bible.

Hezekiah did not evade his own responsibilities in the matter of contribution. His *"portion"* was the tithe, even as it should have been. The king meant to set an example, which he did!

Whenever the church is on fire for God, money is given liberally to the work of God; otherwise, there is little giving. When we give in *"heaps,"* the Lord gives it back to us even in greater heaps (Lk. 6:38).

In the *"third month,"* the Feast of Pentecost was conducted, while in the *"seventh month,"* the Feast of Tabernacles was conducted.

BURNT OFFERINGS AND PEACE OFFERINGS

If it is to be noticed, whenever Judah strayed from the Lord, the sacrifices ceased, or if they did continue, it was only a matter of ceremony. When Judah was on its way back to the Lord, the first thing that was reinstituted was always the sacrificial system. The sacrificial system actually began at the very dawn of time. We find the first account given in Chapter 4 of Genesis as it regarded Cain and Abel. It continued to be conducted more or less even unto the flood and was picked up again by Noah after the flood (Gen. 8:20). By Noah offering up sacrifice, we find that civilization, as it sprang from the sons of Noah, had as its foundation the Cross of Christ, i.e., the altar.

When this sacrifice was offered, the Scripture says, *"And the LORD smelled a sweet savor* (the burning of the sacrifice was sweet unto the Lord because it spoke of the coming Redeemer, who would lift man out of this morass of evil)" (Gen. 8:21) (The Expositor's Study Bible).

The sacrificial system continued under Abraham. In fact, Abraham built so many altars on which to offer sacrifice that he was referred to as the altar builder (Gen. 12:7-8; 13:4, 18; 22:9).

When the law was given, the very core or heartbeat of the law was the sacrificial system. Were it not for that system, Israel could not have survived. Their only recourse was the altar, i.e., the Cross.

THE ALTAR

As is obvious, the altar typified the Cross of Calvary, and the offering up of the clean animals on that altar previewed the coming Redeemer, who would be the Lord Jesus Christ, who would give His life as a ransom for many. When Jesus came, of course, the altar and the sacrificial system were no longer needed. The sacrificial system was always a shadow of that which was to come. Now that the substance has come, the Lord Jesus Christ, His one sacrifice of Himself sufficed then and will suffice for all of eternity. In fact, Paul referred to it as the *"everlasting covenant"* (Heb. 13:20).

It has not changed presently. The only thing standing between mankind and the judgment of God is the Cross of Christ. In fact, the only thing standing between the church and apostasy is the Cross of Christ. Whenever the church leaves the Cross, it always goes into apostasy. I'm afraid that I have to say at present, and certainly with no gladness of heart, that the church is not merely on the road of apostasy, it has already apostatized, and it's because it has left the Cross.

Hezekiah appointed the priests their rightful courses in order that they may continually offer burnt offerings and peace offerings *"and to give thanks, and to praise in the gates of the tents of the LORD."*

THE LAW OF THE LORD

As it regards Hezekiah and his obedience to the Word, the latter portion of verse 3 says, *"As it is written in the law of the LORD."*

In other words, the king was doing everything in his power to abide by the written Word of God.

The Word of God is the single most important thing in the entirety of the world. In fact, the Bible is the only revealed truth in the world and, in fact, ever has been.

I did not say that the Bible is the only thing that is true, but rather that it is the only "truth." Concerning truth, the Scripture says:

- Jesus is truth. He doesn't merely have truth, He is truth (Jn. 14:6).

- The Word of the Lord is truth (Jn. 17:17).

- The Holy Spirit is truth (I Jn. 5:6).

IS ALL TRUTH GOD'S TRUTH?

Yes, it is!

However, one must first know what truth actually is. As stated, just because something is true, it doesn't mean at all that it is truth. For instance, it is true that if one drinks enough alcohol, one will be drunk, but that most definitely isn't truth.

One particular preacher of my acquaintance claimed that it was God who gave to Freud the rudiments of humanistic psychology. He claimed this on the basis of *"all truth is God's truth."* Our dear brother evidently did not really know what truth actually was or is.

We might say that truth is not a philosophy. In fact, philosophy is the search for truth. Truth is rather a person, and we speak of the Lord Jesus Christ. The same thing can be said of the Holy Spirit.

As well, the Word of God, which is truth, is the written form of the living Word, the Lord Jesus Christ. If it is to be noticed, everything that Jesus did in His earthly ministry was backed up totally by the Word of God. In other words, He did nothing outside of the Word.

THE BIBLE

As we have said previously, Satan is presently making possibly his greatest attack against the Word of God; however, he is doing it in a subtle way. He's not making the attack from a frontal position, but rather, one might say, an end run. He is not directly opposing the Word of God but merely perverting the Word of God. He is doing such by bringing out scores of books that claim to be Bibles, such as *The Message Bible,* which are merely collections of religious thoughts by some individuals. Please read the next lines very carefully.

Unless your Bible is a word-for-word translation, then it's really not a Bible but merely a religious book. Most of the so-called Bibles at the present time come under the category of religious books. In other words, it's not the Bible because it's not a word-for-word translation.

The King James Bible is a word-for-word translation, and there are one or two others as well. The King James Version is what we recommend. Dr. Kenneth Wuest, a noted Greek scholar of the 20TH century, stated, and I concur, "When you hold the King James Bible in your hands, you can be certain that you are holding in your hands the Word of God."

Concerning how important all of this is, Jesus said, *"Man shall not live by bread alone, but by every Word that proceeds out of the mouth of God"* (Mat. 4:4).

THE MANNER IN WHICH THE WORD OF GOD WAS WRITTEN

Christians should understand that when the Word of God was originally given, actually covering a timespan of approximately 1,600 years (from the time of Moses and concluding with John the Beloved, who closed out the canon of Scripture by writing the book of Revelation), the writers of the

Gospels—Matthew, Mark, Luke, and John—did not write the words of Christ in red. In fact, there was no red ink at that time.

As well, they did not write the sacred text in Elizabethan English. That type of English was given to us by the King James translators several hundred years ago. In fact, the King James translation has undergone several rewrites, and rightly so. I have a copy of the King James translation, and it would be very difficult, if not nearly impossible, for anyone presently to read it.

THE KING JAMES BIBLE

I'm addressing this because some Christians have in their minds that if it's not Elizabethan English, then it's not the Bible. The Old Testament writers wrote in Hebrew, while the New Testament writers wrote in Greek.

When the King James translators performed their great work, they used the English of that time, which is all they could do, and rightly so. From then until now, some of the words have changed meanings, and if the opportunity presents itself, we should effect that change of meaning in present printings, that is, if possible.

For instance Peter said, *"Forasmuch as you know that you were not redeemed with corruptible things, as silver and gold, from your vain conversation received by tradition from your fathers"* (I Pet. 1:18).

The word *conversation* translated thusly by the King James translators had an entirely different meaning then than it does now. Then, it meant one's lifestyle or the manner of one's behavior. Now, it refers to two or more people conversing with each other.

As stated, through the centuries, some words have changed meanings; however, in truth, not that many words in the King James have changed.

I think it can be said without fear of contradiction, which I've already stated, that when one holds the King James Version in one's hand, one can understand that one is truly holding in his hand the Word of God.

THE ABUNDANCE

When the Spirit of the Lord is moving, which always takes place when people adhere to the Word of God, then everything starts to move in a positive way, and there is an abundance. When people love the Lord, and they are trying to function according to the Word of God, their giving becomes automatic. They realize what the Lord has done for them, and they want to reciprocate as best they can. Of course, we cannot earn anything from the Lord, and neither can we pay for anything that we receive from the Lord. In fact, the Lord has nothing for sale. Everything He has comes in the form of a gift, and, in reality, there are no strings attached. He only asks that we love Him and strive to obey Him to the best of our ability.

In fact, as it regards this, Jesus said, *"My yoke is easy, and My burden is light"* (Mat. 11:30). In other words, the Lord doesn't demand very much of us. Actually, He demands almost nothing as it compares to what Satan demands of his followers. It's truly a pleasure to live for the Lord; it's truly a pleasure to follow Him; and it's truly a pleasure to know Him.

HEAPS

During the time of Judah's existence, they tithed their corn, their wine, their oil, their honey, etc. In other words, they brought in a tenth of their crop and deposited it at the temple to be used by the priests, for this was a part of the upkeep for the priests. They brought so much that it was labeled as *"heaps,"* and rightly so!

Under the new covenant, virtually all of the giving is in the form of money, as would be obvious. Actually, there are two things that are predominant as it regards giving:

1. We are obligated as believers to give to the work of God. Paul said that we should give to show the sincerity of our love (II Cor. 8:8). If we say we love the Lord and, in fact, actually do, we will give to His work. It's that simple! As far as I am concerned, people who will not give to the work of God simply need to get saved. Anyone who is truly saved knows what the Lord has done for him, which constitutes an appreciation and a love for God that knows no bounds and desires that others may know also.

EVERY BELIEVER MUST GIVE

Any believer who claims he cannot afford to give is cheating himself. The way to get out of poverty and, in fact, the only way for the believer to get out of poverty is to start giving to the Lord. The old adage is true that we simply cannot outgive God. In fact, giving to the Lord must be the first thing in our budget. Everything else must take second or third place.

Jesus plainly told us, *"But seek you first the kingdom of God, and His righteousness* (this gives the 'condition' for God's blessings; His interests are to be 'first'); a*nd all these things shall be added unto you* (this is the 'guarantee' of God's provision)*"* (Mat. 6:33) (The Expositor's Study Bible).

In fact, when a person comes to Christ, he enters into God's economy, which is not affected by the ups and downs of the economy of the world. When the believing sinner comes to Christ, he enters into a brand-new culture, the culture of the Bible, and, as stated, he enters into God's economy. Yes, we are to use good sense in our daily walk, as should be obvious, but we are to look exclusively to the Lord for promotion. As well, as believers and understanding His Word, we are to expect promotion.

BLESSINGS AND INCREASE

Let us say it again: As believers and understanding His Word, we are to expect promotion from the Lord. We are to believe Him for this. In turn, we will put the kingdom of God first, even as Jesus demanded that we do. If that is done, and done with a spirit of expectation, the blessings of God are guaranteed, providing the second point is correct, which we will now address. Incidentally, the word *blessings* means "increase."

2. The second thing that must be done in our giving is to be sure about *where* we give. It is just as important as the fact of our giving. Biblical sense should tell us that if we're supporting that which is not of God, it cannot be blessed by the Lord. In fact, He doesn't even consider it as truly a gift to His work because it isn't His work. Regrettably, most giving falls under that category. While it is certainly incumbent upon every believer to help take the gospel of Jesus Christ and Him crucified to the entirety of the world, still, we must be certain that what we are supporting is "Jesus Christ and Him crucified" and not something else. Part gospel or no gospel at all helps few, but yet, sad to say, that's what most of the modern church is presently supporting.

The idea that we are to give, and whatever is done with that money is now none of our business, could not be more wrong. To be sure, we are responsible to give, but we are responsible to know where we are giving and for what our money is used. Sadly and regrettably, most missionaries presently are amateur psychologists. This means they are not really teaching and preaching the gospel but something else entirely. It should not be supported. In fact, it's the message that must be right, which means that it is thoroughly biblical. Other than that, it's not going to help anyone. Consequently, such must not be supported.

THE APOSTLE PAUL

Let's use a New Testament example. As most Bible students know, Paul's greatest difficulty was the Judaizers who came into the churches that he had planted, seeking to divert the people from grace to law. Actually, Paul didn't have much patience with these false apostles. He said of them, and I quote from The Expositor's Study Bible:

Beware of dogs (the apostle is addressing the Judaizers, who were Jews from Jerusalem who claimed Christ but insisted on believers keeping the law as well; all of this was diametrically opposed to Paul's gospel of grace, in which the law of Moses had no part; as well, by the use of the word 'dogs,' the apostle was using the worst slur), *beware of evil workers* (they denigrated the Cross), *beware of the concision.* (This presents a Greek word Paul uses as a play upon the Greek word 'circumcision,' which was at the heart of the law gospel of the Judaizers) (Phil. 3:2).

SATAN'S MINISTERS

The great apostle also said:

For such are false apostles, deceitful workers (they have no rightful claim to the apostolic office; they are deceivers), *transforming themselves into the apostles of Christ.* (They have called themselves to this office.) *And no marvel* (true believers should not be surprised); *for Satan himself is transformed into an angel of light.* (This means he pretends to be that which he is not.) *Therefore it is no great thing if his ministers* (Satan's ministers) *also be transformed as the ministers of righteousness* (despite their claims, they were 'Satan's ministers' because they preached something other than the Cross [I Cor. 1:17-18, 21, 23; 2:2; Gal. 1:8-9]); *whose end shall be according to their works* (that 'end' is spiritual destruction [Phil. 3:18-19]) (II Cor. 11:13-15) (The Expositor's Study Bible).

Now, I'll ask the question: Is it permissible to support these false apostles—those whom the Holy Spirit through Paul labeled as "dogs," etc.? I think the answer to that would be an obvious no! And yet, most of what is being presently supported, and more than likely it's always been that way, is that which falls into the category of "false." The Lord does not label such as true giving, as ought to be obvious.

TO WHAT SHOULD WE GIVE?

As it regards that, the Holy Spirit through the apostle Paul gave us implicit direction as well.

When Paul was in prison in Rome, Epaphroditus came from the church at Philippi, a distance of nearly 1,000 miles, and brought to Paul a very generous offering from that particular church. Paul's epistle known as "Philippians," which was sent back to the church, was, among other things, a thank you note for their generosity to him, which was very much needed.

Paul said:

Notwithstanding you have well done, that you did communicate with my affliction. (They helped Paul with his needs as it regarded the offering they sent him.) *Now you Philippians know also, that in the beginning of the gospel,* (refers to the time when Paul first preached the Word to them, about ten years previously), *when I departed from Macedonia, no church communicated with me as concerning giving and receiving, but you only* (proclaims the fact that the Philippians had always been generous). *For even in Thessalonica* (when he was starting the church there) *you sent once and again unto my necessity* (proclaims their faithfulness).

THE CROSS

Not because I desire a gift (presents the apostle defending himself against the slanderous assertion that he is using the gospel as a means to make money): *but I desire fruit that may abound to your account.* (God keeps a record of everything, even our gifts, whether giving or receiving.) *But I have all, and abound: I am full* (proclaims the fact that the Philippian gift must have been generous), *having received of Epaphroditus the things which were sent from you* (Epaphroditus had brought the gift from Philippi to Rome), *an odor of a sweet smell* (presents the Old Testament odors of the Levitical sacrifices, all typifying Christ), *a sacrifice acceptable, well-pleasing to God.* (For those who gave to Paul, enabling him to take the

Message of the Cross to others, their gift, and such gifts presently, are looked at by God as a part of the sacrificial atoning work of Christ on the Cross. Nothing could be higher than that!) *But my God shall supply all your need* (presents the apostle assuring the Philippians and all other believers, as well, that they have not impoverished themselves in giving so liberally to the cause of Christ) *according to His riches in glory* (the measure of supply will be determined by the wealth of God in glory) *by Christ Jesus* (made possible by the Cross) (Phil. 4:14-19) (The Expositor's Study Bible.)

Pure and simple, the only giving that God recognizes as such is that which is given to help proclaim the Message of the Cross, which is the meaning of the new covenant, to a hurting and dying world.

AN ODOR OF A SWEET SMELL

Two things are said here by the Holy Spirit as it regards the statements given by the apostle.

First of all, the great apostle likened the gift given to him as *"an odor of a sweet smell."* What did he mean by that?

This statement, or one similar, was often used as it regarded sacrifices of clean animals offered up to the Lord. You'll find the statement in Genesis 8:20-21; Ezra 6:10; Exodus 29:18; and Leviticus 1:9, 13, 17; 2:2, 9, 12; 3:5, 16.

How could an animal burning on an altar with greasy smoke going up toward heaven present itself as a sweet savor unto the Lord? It could and did simply because it typified the Son of God giving Himself on the altar of sacrifice, i.e., the Cross, which would redeem humanity from the terrible morass of evil. That's why it was a sweet savor—a sweet odor unto the Lord.

THE CROSS

As should be obvious, all of this pertained to the Cross. As we have repeatedly stated, the meaning of the new covenant is the meaning of the Cross. It is the gospel of good news; it is the means of salvation for the sinner and sanctification for the saint. If the preacher is not preaching that, then whatever it is he is preaching is not the gospel.

Paul also stated as he wrote to the Galatians:

I marvel that you are so soon removed from Him (the Holy Spirit) who called you into the grace of Christ (made possible by the Cross) *unto another gospel* (anything which doesn't have the Cross as its object of faith): *Which is not another* (presents the fact that Satan's aim is not so much to deny the gospel, which he can little do, as to corrupt it); *but there be some who trouble you, and would pervert the gospel of Christ* (once again, to make the object of faith something other than the Cross). *But though we* (Paul and his associates), *or an angel from heaven, preach any other gospel unto you than that which we have preached unto you* (Jesus Christ and Him crucified), *let him be accursed* (eternally condemned; the Holy Spirit speaks this through Paul, making this very serious). *As we said before, so say I now again* (at some time past, he had said the same thing to them, making their defection even more serious), *If any man preach any other gospel unto you* (anything other than the Cross) *than that you have received* (which saved your souls), *let him be accursed* ('eternally condemned,' which means the loss of the soul) (Gal. 1:6-9) (The Expositor's Study Bible).

WHAT IS THE GOSPEL?

In fact, Paul also told us exactly what the gospel of Jesus Christ actually is. He said: *"For Christ sent me not to baptize* (presents to us a cardinal truth), *but to preach the gospel* (the manner in which one may be saved from sin): *not with wisdom of words* (intellectualism is not the gospel), *lest the Cross of Christ should be made of none effect.* (This tells us in no uncertain terms that the Cross of Christ must always be the emphasis of the message)" (I Cor. 1:17) (The Expositor's Study Bible).

As well, it tells us that the gospel is the Message of the Cross. Let me say it again: Unless one is supporting the Message of the Cross, whatever it is he is supporting, it's not the gospel. It might be something about the gospel, but unless one is preaching the Cross, one is not really preaching the gospel of Jesus Christ. As well, if it's not the gospel, it should not be supported.

THE LORD HAS BLESSED HIS PEOPLE

And Azariah the chief priest of the house of Zadok answered him, and said, Since the people began to bring the offerings into the house of the LORD, *we have had enough to eat, and have left plenty: for the* LORD *has blessed His people; and that which is left is this great store. Then Hezekiah commanded to prepare chambers in the house of the* LORD; *and they prepared them, and brought in the offerings and the tithes and the dedicated things faithfully: over which Cononiah the Levite was ruler, and Shimei his brother was the next. And Jehiel, and Azaziah, and Nahath, and Asahel, and Jerimoth, and Jozabad, and Eliel, and Ismachiah, and Mahath, and Benaiah, were overseers under the hand of Cononiah and Shimei his brother, at the commandment of Hezekiah the king, and Azariah the ruler of the house of God. And Kore the son of Imnah the Levite, the porter toward the east, was over the freewill offerings of God, to distribute the oblations of the* LORD, *and the most holy things. And next him were Eden, and Miniamin, and Jeshua, and Shemaiah, Amariah, and Shecaniah, in the cities of the priests, in their set office, to give to their brethren by courses, as well to the great as to the small.*

THAT WHICH WAS GOOD AND RIGHT

Beside their genealogy of males, from three years old and upward, even unto everyone who entered into the house of the LORD, *his daily portion for their service in their charges according to their courses; both to the genealogy of the priests by the house of their fathers, and the Levites from twenty years old and upward, in their charges by their courses; and to the genealogy of all their little ones, their wives, and their sons, and their daughters, through all the congregation: for in their set office they sanctified themselves in holiness: Also of the sons of Aaron the priests, which were in the fields of the suburbs of their cities, and every several city, the men who were expressed by name, to give portions to all the males among the priests, and to all who were reckoned by genealogies among the Levites. And thus did Hezekiah throughout all Judah, and wrought that which was good and right and truth before the LORD his God. And in every work that he began in the service of the house of God, and in the law, and in the Commandments, to seek his God, he did it with all his heart, and prospered* (II Chron. 31:10-21).

A GREAT STORE

Under the new covenant, we have even greater promises. If the work of the Lord is put first, the Lord has promised that a "great store" will accrue to us as well (Mat. 6:33).

The latter phrase of verse 15 portrays the fact that in the past, the obligation had not always been honestly discharged.

A picture of the little children being fed for the sake of their father's sanctuary service is a pleasant glimpse.

All of the information given us in these passages given, proclaims the fact that all the priests and the Levites were remembered and carefully provided for, which was the way it was supposed to be.

True prosperity can only be found in faithfully following the Word of the Lord. This Hezekiah did!

WORKERS FOR THE LORD HONORED

Concerning these individuals so named in the sacred text in their work for the Lord, Williams said: "Those who yielded themselves to God to be His instruments in this Reformation were enriched, glorified – enriched by the abounding tithes and glorified by their names being inscribed upon the Sacred Record. Such is God's way with His servants, that we enjoy the blessing and share the glory."

These are sample proofs of the record that God keeps as it regards all of His people and our doings, whatever those doings might be. We should never forget this and understand that the Lord sees, watches, observes, looks, and knows all things.

As well, every believer should understand that one day, each of us will stand at the judgment seat of Christ.

THE JUDGMENT SEAT OF CHRIST

Paul said:

Wherefore we labor (are ambitious), *that, whether present* (with Christ) *or absent* (still in this world), *we may be accepted of Him* (approved by Him, which we will be if our faith is in Christ and the Cross). *For we must all appear before the judgment seat of Christ* (this will take place in heaven and will probably transpire immediately before the second coming)*; that every one may receive the things done in his body, according to that he has done, whether it be good or bad.* (This concerns our life lived for the Lord. Sins will not be judged here, but rather our motivation and faithfulness, for sin was judged at Calvary) (II Cor. 5:9-10) (The Expositor's Study Bible).

As stated, no sins will be judged at the judgment seat of Christ, that already having been taken care of at Calvary. As well, only believers, as should be obvious, will appear at this judgment seat. All unbelievers will appear at the great white throne judgment (Rev. 20:11-15).

The Holy Spirit listed, in this chapter, all of those who were in authority as it regarded the work of the Lord respecting the temple, and they are listed in a positive manner. As we've already stated, respecting all that we do, every single believer is listed accordingly in *"the book"* (Rev. 20:12). Understanding that and realizing that perpetually, we should desire to obey the Lord in all things.

HOLINESS

The holiness referred to in Old Testament times, as is referred to in II Chronicles 31:18, was more ceremonial than anything else. In other words, the individual involved, whomever it may have been, was to do his best to adhere to the law of Moses in every capacity as far as he was able to do so. Due to the blood of bulls and goats being unable to take away sins, the sin debt remained. This means that the Holy Spirit, who alone can perfect holiness in one's heart and life, was unable to function in full capacity. So, as stated, holiness was basically ceremonial.

Since the Cross, holiness now is entirely different. Because of what Jesus did at the Cross in taking our sin away (Jn. 1:29), the Holy Spirit can now live permanently in our hearts and lives, which He does in all believers (Jn. 14:16-18).

LET'S SEE WHAT HOLINESS ISN'T

Holiness is not material things that we do or do not do. In other words, no human being, even the godliest among us, can make himself or herself holy. In an attempt to do such, the only thing that will develop in one's life is self-righteousness.

Holiness is the faith that the believer has in Christ and what Christ did at the Cross. With the Cross of Christ ever being the object of our faith, and continuing to be the object of our faith, the Holy Spirit, who alone can develop His fruit within our lives, can then accomplish His work. So, one might say that holiness is a state of the heart, but the heart is right only because one's faith is right, or rather has the correct object.

The bane of the modern church is, and has always been, at least among some, that holiness is labeled according to material objects in which one does or does not engage. Please understand that one is not holy because one wears certain types of clothing, cuts his hair in a certain way, or engages in particular practices. As stated, all that does is produce self-righteousness.

If the Holy Spirit can have His way in one's life, He will develop holiness in such a heart and life. He can have His way if our faith is properly placed in the Cross of Christ, which, at the same time, says it's anchored squarely in the Word. If the faith of the believer is anchored in something other than the Cross of Christ, that means that such a believer is living in a state of spiritual adultery. To be sure, even though that person is saved, holiness most definitely is not being developed in such a life, as should be obvious.

PERSONAL EFFORTS ...

The believer must come to the place that he realizes that this tremendous attribute of God cannot be developed by one's own personal efforts. In other words, no one can become holy by one's own ability, strength, religiosity, etc. It is impossible! Concerning this, Paul said:

And if Christ be in you (He is in you through the power and person of the Spirit [Gal. 2:20]), the body is dead because of sin (means that the physical body has been rendered helpless because of the fall; consequently, the believer trying to overcome by willpower presents a fruitless task); but the Spirit is life because of righteousness (only the Holy Spirit can make us what we ought to be, which means we cannot do it ourselves; once again, He performs all that He does within the confines of the finished work of Christ) (Rom. 8:10) (The Expositor's Study Bible).

Resting on the faithfulness of Christ our Lord,
Resting on the fullness of His own sure Word,
Resting on His wisdom, on His love and power,
Resting on His covenant from hour to hour.

Resting 'neath His guiding hand for untracked days,
Resting 'neath His shadow from the noontide rays,
Resting at the eventide beneath His wing,
In the fair pavilion of our Saviour King.

Resting in the fortress while the foe is nigh,
Resting in the lifeboat while the waves roll high,
Resting in His chariot for the swift, glad race,
Resting always resting, in His boundless grace.

Resting in the pastures and beneath the Rock,
Resting by the waters where He leads His flock,
Resting while we listen, at His glorious feet,
Resting in His very arms, oh, rest complete!

Resting and believing, let us onward press;
Resting on Himself, the Lord our righteousness;
Resting and rejoicing, let His saved ones sing,
Glory, glory, glory be to Christ our King!

HEZEKIAH

CHAPTER 4

SENNACHERIB

SENNACHERIB

"Now it came to pass in the fourteenth year of king Hezekiah, that Sennacherib king of Assyria came up against all the defenced cities of Judah, and took them" (Isa. 36:1).

SENNACHERIB, THE KING OF ASSYRIA

This is the third time the Holy Spirit records the facts relating to Hezekiah and the proposed attack by Assyria against Jerusalem, thereby, denoting its vast significance. The other two times are found in II Kings, Chapter 18, and II Chronicles, Chapter 32.

Not only was it extremely important regarding the tremendous miracle performed by the Lord in the sending of an angel who killed 185,000 Assyrian soldiers in one night, but it also symbolically portrays the future Assyrian, i.e., the Antichrist. He also will lay siege to Jerusalem, but he will be foiled by the coming of the Lord.

It should be understood that the prophecies concerning this momentous event regarding the defeat of Sennacherib, king of Assyria, were given prior to this account. In this manner, prophecy and history are brought together, thus exhibiting their correspondence, for prophecy is history foretold, and history is prophecy fulfilled. Whereas the Holy Spirit gave the prophetic announcement in previous chapters, He now gives the actual historical account.

THE HISTORICAL ACCOUNT

Concerning the statement, *"The fourteenth year of King Hezekiah,"* some have noted that there is an irreconcilable difference between this note of time in the passage as it stands and the Assyrian inscriptions. It is said that the fourteenth year of Hezekiah was 714 B.C., and that Sennacherib did not ascend the throne until about nine years later. He did not lead an expedition into Judah until some four years after that, creating a 13-year discrepancy.

If that, in fact, is the case, then one of two things has happened:

1. The Assyrian inscriptions are wrong! Due to embarrassing incidents, of which this certainly was one, heathen monarchs at times altered dates to hide their complicity in the debacle. Therefore, dates cannot always be guaranteed outside of the original manuscripts of the Bible.

2. If the Assyrian inscriptions are correct, then the original Hebrew writing has suffered corruption due to the error

of a copyist, which, at times, happened. If that did happen, the number 14 was substituted for 27.

It is said that Sennacherib captured 46 of the strong cities belonging to Hezekiah, king of Judah. He also captured a countless number of the fortresses and small cities. Actually, he took all of Judah, with the exception of Jerusalem, which God delivered supernaturally.

THE CONDUIT OF THE UPPER POOL

"And the king of Assyria sent Rabshakeh from Lachish to Jerusalem unto King Hezekiah with a great army. And he stood by the conduit of the upper pool in the highway of the fuller's field" (Isa. 36:2).

Rabshakeh seemingly was the head of the Assyrian expedition against Jerusalem. He was there to demand the surrender of Jerusalem. With him was *"a great army."* This seems to be the occasion for the prophecy given in Isaiah, Chapter 22.

The phrase, *"The conduit of the upper pool,"* is the same place Isaiah stood with Ahaz about 28 years before (Isa. 7:3). There is no record in the Assyrian inscriptions of this excursion. The reason is because they never recorded any reverse or defeat. This also lends some credence to the possibility of the date on the Assyrian inscription concerning Sennacherib being altered, as we suggested.

Lachish was a city about 30 miles southwest of Jerusalem. Sennacherib took this city in Judah, of which the account is given on the Assyrian inscriptions presently in the British

Museum in London. By capturing Lachish, Sennacherib prevented any Egyptian assistance reaching Jerusalem, where he sent his messengers to demand Hezekiah's surrender.

The phrase, *"The conduit of the upper pool,"* has to do with the manner in which water was taken into Jerusalem. In fact, Hezekiah made this conduit, which still exists presently. I have personally stood in this conduit, which is carved out of solid rock (II Ki. 20:20).

The chisel marks of the workmen are still visible on the rock.

RABSHAKEH

"Then came forth unto him Eliakim, Hilkiah's son, which was over the house, and Shebna the scribe, and Joah, Asaph's son, the recorder. And Rabshakeh said unto them, Say you now to Hezekiah, Thus says the great king, the king of Assyria, What confidence is this wherein you trust?" (Isa. 36:3-4).

Eliakim and Shebna were sent outside the city to meet with Rabshakeh. This is the same Shebna whom Isaiah prophesied against in Isaiah, Chapter 22.

Hezekiah had rebelled against the king of Assyria by refusing to pay the tribute imposed upon Judah in the days of his father Ahaz (II Ki. 18:7). He had also trusted in Egypt for help against the Assyrians, but that country could not help him.

Of the three Assyrian envoys, only Rabshakeh, who was the spokesman, received mention in Isaiah. He was probably chosen for such because he could speak Hebrew fluently. Rabshakeh referred to the king of Assyria as *"the great king."* This is meant to insinuate that no other king anywhere in the world was as great as the king of Assyria. However, Rabshakeh would find to his dismay that his King Sennacherib was subservient to another king—the Lord of glory.

CONTEMPT FOR JERUSALEM

"I say, say you, (but they are but vain words) I have counsel and strength for war: now on whom do you trust, that you rebel against me? Lo, you trust in the staff of this broken reed, on Egypt; whereon if a man lean, it will go into his hand, and pierce it: so is Pharaoh king of Egypt to all who trust in him" (Isa. 36:5-6).

It seems that Rabshakeh had obtained a copy of the proposed agreement between Judah and Egypt, or that the very words had been reported to him. The entirety of the following harangue by Rabshakeh shows his contempt for Jerusalem, Hezekiah, and those on whom Judah trusted, namely Egypt. The Assyrians could afford to bluster, for their victories up till then had been constant; consequently, he would toy with Jerusalem and Hezekiah, as a cat toys with a mouse.

When the Assyrian spoke of this *"broken reed,"* namely Egypt, he was speaking from the position of knowledge instead of merely boasting.

THE ARM OF FLESH

Not so many years before, Egypt had been mighty, perhaps at that time, the greatest and most powerful nation in the world.

Now it was fragmented and weakened, in other words, a *"broken reed."* At this time, the Ethiopians ruled much of the Nile valley, with lackey princes ruling particular portions. So, when Rabshakeh spoke of *"Pharaoh, king of Egypt,"* he was making a generalized statement.

What knowledge Judah had of Egypt's present weakness is not known; nevertheless, the analogy should be well taken. The arm of flesh, whether weak or strong, must never be leaned upon by the child of God. If it is a weak arm, its uselessness is obvious, but a strong arm will exact such a high price for its help that it will be unaffordable.

THE LORD OF GLORY

Furthermore, the Lord of glory, in His planned instruction and training, allows certain vicissitudes in order that we may learn trust in God. For us to foil such by failing to go to Him— by our leaning rather on the arm of flesh—totally abrogates His methods and plans. Perhaps this is the reason there are so many weak Christians!

Let the following be clearly understood: If the believer doesn't understand the Cross of Christ as it refers to sanctification—how we live for God and how we order our behavior— invariably such a believer, and without exception, will lean on the arm of flesh. The only way one can lean on the arm of the Lord is to function according to God's way, His prescribed order, which is Christ and Him crucified. Anything and everything else can be chalked up as the arm of flesh.

THE IGNORANCE OF THE WORLD

"But if you say to me, We trust in the Lord our God: is it not He, whose high places and whose altars Hezekiah has taken away, and said to Judah and to Jerusalem, You shall worship before this altar?" (Isa. 36:7).

To destroy the fashionable materials and corrupt ceremonies of worldly religion is misunderstood by the world and accounted sacrilege. Rabshakeh was totally ignorant of the ways of God and had misunderstood Hezekiah's destruction of the idol groves, thinking that he had offended the God of Judah. Rabshakeh also, at least at this stage, had no fear of the God of Judah because he knew that the northern kingdom of Israel had also served the same God, or had so after a fashion! The northern kingdom had been totally defeated by the Assyrians and were led away in shame and disgrace.

In Rabshakeh's thinking, if this God did not help Israel, why would He help Judah? In his mind, Assyria's gods were stronger than Israel's or Judah's God. He understood not at all that Israel had been defeated because of her many sins. If she had been serving God as she should have been, then no nation in the world, including Assyria, could have defeated her! Rabshakeh, being ignorant of all of this, now approached Judah.

THE BRAZEN ALTAR

When he spoke of worshipping before *"this altar,"* he was speaking of the brazen altar in the great court of the temple.

Hezekiah had cleansed it from the pollutions of the time of his father Ahaz (Isa. 29:18), and had insisted on sacrifices being offered nowhere else (II Chron. 29:21-25; 30:15-24; 31:1).

Such a concentration of worship was unknown to any of the heathen nations. It was undoubtedly unintelligible to them. Israel was, in fact, the only nation in the world, at that time, that was monotheistic, meaning they worshipped one God. All the other nations of the world were polytheistic.

As Rabshakeh saw the smoke going up from this altar, he little understood the divine meaning! He did not realize that this brazen altar was a type of Calvary and was a symbol of power that was totally unimaginable to him. Therefore, he would speak of it sarcastically.

BLASPHEMY

Having no clue that the One of whom they are speaking holds the very breath in His hands, the world speaks of Christ and the Holy Spirit with acute glibness and shocking irreverence! It is only the grace of God that keeps the world from instant doom. Most of modern literature and entertainment is not only an affront to the Lord of glory but is outright blasphemy.

Not too long ago in the modern rock 'n' roll music scene, a song was written entitled "Big Daddy and Little Spook." The song was referring to God the Father and God the Holy Spirit.

Jesus said, *"All manner of sin and blasphemy shall be forgiven unto men: but the blasphemy against the Holy Spirit shall not be forgiven unto men"* (Mat. 12:31).

Is it possible that America as a nation is coming close to blaspheming the Holy Spirit?

Sometime back, I was preaching a crusade in a major American city. One night after the service, I had gone to our hotel room to get something and then started back downstairs to meet Frances and others. I got off the elevator on the main floor and walked down a long hall, where I overheard Christian music. The song was, "Just a Closer Walk With Thee."

WHY?

When I drew abreast of the door from where the sound emanated, I pushed open the door to see what was happening inside. To my surprise, and dismay, it was not worship, but rather a party. Liquor bottles littered the tables, and couples were gliding across the dance floor. For a moment, I stood there in shock. Why did they have to use a sacred song for their partying?

Regrettably and sadly, that which was a shock to me some years ago is now commonplace. And why not, especially when we consider that so-called Christian contemporary music is identical to its ungodly counterpart? Actually, both are ungodly!

America has lost its respect for the things of God. Anything pertaining to the Lord, Christianity, or the Bible cannot be used in any government building or public school. We no longer have separation of church and state, which is correct, but rather separation of God and state!

It is because the church has also lost its respect for the things of God.

For the obvious reasons, Rabshakeh had no respect for the God of Judah. The world today has no respect for the church, and for the same obvious reasons!

WHO IS THE MASTER, GOD OR SATAN?

"Now therefore give pledges, I pray you, to my master the king of Assyria, and I will give you two thousand horses, if you be able on your part to set riders upon them" (Isa. 36:8).

Rabshakeh continued to reproach Judah. He instructed Judah to acquiesce to his demands and give a *"pledge to the king of Assyria."*

He then proceeded to further make light of Judah's military power. He offered to give them two thousand horses if they could find capable riders to put on them. He said this knowing Judah's impotence. At the same time, he was, no doubt, thinking of the tens of thousands of cavalrymen that his own army possessed.

In this statement, the efforts of Satan become obvious. He is a serious master, and he wanted to be Judah's master as well.

The fiery trials and tests that come to believers are allowed by God, yet much of the time, they are designed by Satan. Satan strongly desires to be our master. Each test, at least in part, is for the explicit purpose of ascertaining what master we will serve!

In the spirit world, the die is cast on that front. Who will be our master—God or Satan?

Jesus said, *"No man can serve two masters"* (Mat. 6:24).

THE SIN NATURE AND THE BELIEVER

Actually, we've already dealt with the sin nature in this volume, but due to the tremendous significance of this subject, please allow this short repetition.

If the Christian doesn't understand the sin nature—and most don't—which means he doesn't understand the Cross, then the sin nature will rule such a Christian as it does virtually all Christians presently. Then, at least to a great degree, Satan is their master.

If a believer is dominated by any sin, then he is not free. To be sure, if the believer doesn't understand the Cross as it refers to sanctification, then, in some way, *"a work"* or *"works of the flesh"* will manifest themselves in him (Gal. 5:19-21).

So, in modern Christendom (and to a certain degree, this has always existed), there are individuals who truly love the Lord, and who are doing their very best to serve Him. However, they are being overrun by the *"god"* of this present world because they do not understand God's prescribed order of victory, which is the Cross of Christ (II Cor. 4:4; Rom. 6:1-14; Gal. 6:14; Col. 2:10-15).

SATAN'S THREATS

"How then will you turn away the face of one captain of the least of my master's servants, and put your trust on Egypt for chariots and for horsemen?" (Isa. 36:9).

Rabshakeh was telling Hezekiah and Judah that if they chose to fight, they could not even turn him away, as he likened

himself to *"one captain."* He then referred to the many captains
of the vast army of Assyria. Then he again spoke of Egypt.
Actually, Egypt had sent a large force to the help of Ekron a
short time previously. That force, however, had suffered defeat
at the hands of Sennacherib; therefore, Rabshakeh continued
to mock Judah's weakness.

Judah's true weakness was not her lack of military preparedness, but rather her lack of dependence upon God. Today our
weakness is the same. Judah had no hope, in the natural, of
defeating Assyria, and we, likewise, have no hope in the natural
of defeating Satan. Satan's power is so much greater than ours
that it beggars description. Judah's only hope was God, and our
only hope, likewise, is God.

THE POWER OF SATAN

The modern Christian little knows or understands the terrible force and power of Satan. Satan's power is so great that
it was necessary for God to become man and die on a cruel
Cross in order to rescue man from the terrible clutches of the
Evil One. In other words, only God could do such!

Now don't misunderstand. Satan is a creature, who was
created by God. Of course, when he was created, Satan was
created righteous and holy, in which state he functioned for an
undetermined period of time. However, despite his power, he
is still a creature, meaning he was created by the Creator.

On the other hand, God is omnipotent, which means that
He is all-powerful. To be sure, Satan falls far below such power,

which should be obvious, but man still is no match for Satan, at least on our own terms. We can defeat him, but only if we subscribe to God's prescribed order, which is the Cross of Christ and our faith in that matchless sacrifice.

This is what makes it so ridiculous for Christians to lean on the frail arm of flesh, i.e., psychologists and so-called counselors. There is no help from that source, even as there has never been any help from that source. Our help comes from the Lord, or else, no help is available!

UNCONVERTED MEN IN THE BIBLE

"And am I now come up without the Lord against this land to destroy it? the Lord said unto me, Go up against this land, and destroy it" (Isa. 36:10).

Rabshakeh's statements make it obvious that he has read or seen the prophecy given by Isaiah some years before. The use by Rabshakeh of the prophecy of Isaiah was a clever ruse to persuade the people to disobey Jehovah, but in verse 20, Rabshakeh contradicts his own statement made here about the Lord telling him to do thus and so.

When unconverted men quote the Bible in support of their projects or doctrines, they contradict themselves and expose both their ignorance of the Scriptures and their hatred of God.

Sennacherib and his captain, Rabshakeh, did not believe in Jehovah. Their statements were made from the viewpoint of ego. They imagined themselves to be so high and mighty that if there actually is a God, they were His princely ones in the earth.

FACE-TO-FACE WITH GOD

In fact, Sennacherib misunderstood Isaiah's prophecy. It was true that God did use the Assyrians to do certain things (but without their knowledge because God was working behind the scenes); still, He did not charge them to destroy Judah. God did allow them to destroy the northern kingdom of Israel, but Judah was not included; consequently, they were overstepping their bounds and were about to come face-to-face with God. The situation would definitely not turn out as they imagined!

WHO WAS SENNACHERIB?

Sennacherib was the head of the mighty Assyrian Empire, which he ruled for a little more than 20 years. While he had little trouble defeating army after army of those who opposed him, when he came up against Judah, he came up against something that was beyond his power to even begin to comprehend. He came up against the power of Almighty God. The account of his defeat, which was carried out by just one angel, is given to us three times in the Bible. It is given in II Kings, beginning with Chapter 18, and in II Chronicles, beginning with Chapter 32. As well, the account is given by the great Prophet Isaiah, beginning with Chapter 36 of his great book.

THE CONTRAST

"Then said Eliakim and Shebna and Joah unto Rabshakeh, Speak, I pray you, unto your servants in the Syrian language; for we understand it: and speak not to us in the Jews' language, in the ears of the people who are on the wall" (Isa. 36:11).

The use here of the word *Jew* is interesting because it is about this time that the word began to be used for the Israelite people. The first use was under King Ahaz, the father of Hezekiah, which was a few years earlier (II Ki. 16:6).

The Syrian language literally was the Aramaic language.

Rabshakeh spoke in Hebrew because he wanted the people, as well as the leaders, to hear his word. His purpose in doing this was so that their will to resist would be weakened. He ignored the request by the Jews that he not do this.

Three Jews are addressed here, and two of them, Eliakim and Shebna, are strongly contrasted. Eliakim is a type of Christ; hence, he is symbolic of the Spirit. Shebna is a type of Satan; hence, he is a type of the flesh (Isa. 22:15-24). Shebna strongly encouraged seeking the help of the Egyptians, while Eliakim strongly urged trust in God. So it is with the modern church!

SHEBNA AND ELIAKIM

In Jerusalem of that time, the far greater majority followed Shebna, and a small remnant followed Isaiah and Eliakim (Isa. 1:9). Almost all of the religious leaders of Jerusalem followed the carnal path of Shebna.

Why?

These individuals, which made up the far greater majority, had no concern about God's will. They only desired accommodations that would allow them to continue their pursuit of riches and worldly pleasures. They cared little about a coming Messiah. The promises of God made to David so long ago held no interest for them. In other words, self-will was their master, i.e., Satan.

The great prophet Isaiah, Eliakim, and Hezekiah, along with a small remnant, desired to please God and His will to be carried out; however, there is strong evidence that even Hezekiah was strongly swayed by Shebna and his ilk, at least in the beginning (Isa., Chpts. 30-31).

THREATS!

"But Rabshakeh said, Has my master sent me to your master and to you to speak these words? has he not sent me to the men who sit upon the wall, that they may eat their own dung, and drink their own urine with you?" (Isa. 36:12).

The language used by Rabshakeh showed his contempt for Judah.

Rabshakeh was saying that if Judah did not yield to him, they would be reduced to the utter extremity of famine when the siege began. His threats were powerful, and they, no doubt, had their intended effect upon the hearers.

These were not empty threats. Judah had a choice: They could trust in Egypt, themselves, surrender, or trust God.

They were not without promise. Isaiah's prophecies had been explicit. They were admonished to trust God.

As the scenario concerning Judah and Assyria played out that day so long ago before the host of heaven, likewise, it plays out no differently today. Judah then had the prophecies of Isaiah, while we now have the prophecies of Isaiah, as well as the entirety of the Bible. Even though each situation is relative, still, the test for every Christian is the same. Will we listen to the threats of Satan and acquiesce to him, or will we trust God?

A PERSONAL EXPERIENCE

"Then Rabshakeh stood, and cried with a loud voice in the Jews' language, and said, Hear you the words of the great king, the king of Assyria" (Isa. 36:13).

Satan always cries with a loud voice. He also says it in language that we easily understand. As this played out so long ago, it was but a picture or a symbol of the spiritual battles that we fight presently.

If I remember correctly, it was the latter part of 1992. I faced an example in miniature of that which we are now studying. On that particular day, Satan had made two different thrusts at us, which, at the time, seemed very powerful. A large law firm in a major city had made strong threats against us. I might quickly state that this law firm had ample financial resources. We were totally innocent of any wrongdoing, but, of course, this was of no consequence to them. On the very same day, another situation with a portent of great difficulties had also arisen. To defend ourselves against this would cost untold thousands of dollars—money that we did not have.

That same evening, Frances and I went to our nightly prayer meeting. As I began to pray, these things loomed large in my mind. The more I thought on them, the larger they became. In a short time, my prayer was more of a moan of defeat than of victory. And then the Holy Spirit began to move.

THE HOLY SPIRIT SPEAKS

His power and presence were unmistakable. This is what He said to me: "You are conducting yourself like the 10 unbelieving spies who went into Canaan. When they came back, all they could speak of was the height of the wall surrounding the cities and the giant size of the people. Conversely, they thought of themselves as grasshoppers."

The Holy Spirit continued to speak to my heart and said: "You are doing the same thing. When you look at your problems, they, as the walls and giants, loom larger and larger."

Then He said: "Take your eyes off these things and look to Me. If you will look at Me, I will get larger and larger, while these problems will get smaller and smaller."

Then He gave me this simple truth: "Doubt always exaggerates a problem and minimizes God. Conversely, faith minimizes the problem and magnifies God."

I have never forgotten that night. The presence of the Lord covered me like a cloud. In a few moments of time, it seemed as though these problems melted away. It was as though they were no longer there.

As we were driving home from the prayer meeting, I related what I had experienced to Frances, and I could sense the presence of the Lord literally come into our automobile. That evening when we arrived, we were dragging, so to speak; but when we went home, we were shouting. Such is faith!

Incidentally, the threats of that large law firm proved to be empty, and the other problem was handled without fanfare or expense. Neither situation cost the ministry a single dime. Hallelujah!

THE MODERN CHURCH

"Thus says the king (King Sennacherib), Let not Hezekiah deceive you: for he shall not be able to deliver you" (Isa. 36:14).

Rabshakeh claimed to speak for King Sennacherib. Satan has many envoys. The people had a choice. They could believe either Rabshakeh or Hezekiah. If the people had not had strong spiritual leadership in the persons of the great prophet Isaiah and King Hezekiah, they undoubtedly would have acquiesced to Rabshakeh.

After the fact, it is obvious as to where the real deception lay. Rabshakeh is today in hell, while Hezekiah is in heaven. Even though Hezekiah and Isaiah did not have many followers (a small remnant), their strong spiritual leadership nevertheless was enough to bring great victory to Judah.

As I write these words, the church in America is like sheep that have no shepherd. Their leadership is, by and large, man-given; therefore, they are man-led. For the most part, the headship of Christ has been abrogated by denominationalism.

THE HOLY SPIRIT

In the early 1990s, the general superintendent of the Assemblies of God sent a directive to the district superintendents, urging them to encourage the pastors to "preach on the Holy Spirit." Reports had come into the headquarters that precious few people were being baptized with the Holy Spirit in Assemblies of God churches. A few months later, a report was given in their general counsel that stated that only a little over one-third of Assemblies of God members actually claimed to be baptized with the Holy Spirit with the evidence of speaking with other tongues. Sadly, some, if not many, Assemblies of God preachers no longer believe that speaking with other tongues is the initial physical evidence that one has been baptized with the Holy Spirit.

These things are happening in this once-great denomination for many and varied reasons, but for the most part, it is because the headship of Christ has been replaced by man. Sadly, too many in the religious world are listening to the Assyrian rather than to Hezekiah.

TRUSTING THE LORD

"Neither let Hezekiah make you trust in the Lord, saying, The Lord will surely deliver us: this city shall not be delivered into the hand of the king of Assyria" (Isa. 36:15).

Rabshakeh had, no doubt, reported to Sennacherib the words that Isaiah had given to Hezekiah. Hezekiah would naturally repeat these promises to the people. He could not give their effect in simpler words than by saying, "Jehovah will surely deliver us. This city shall not be delivered into the hand of the king of Assyria." It was the Word of the Lord versus the word of Sennacherib.

Presently, it has little changed!

The people would forever shout the praises of God because they had let Hezekiah make them trust in the Lord.

What does *"trust in the Lord"* mean?

First of all, let's see what it is not: trust in the Lord is not presumption. A man sat on his porch and refused to go to work, claiming that his faith in God would provide for him. In those circumstances, it did not provide and will not provide. God will not do for us what we are supposed to do for ourselves.

Some also have foolishly claimed that inasmuch as Christ is the healer (which He certainly is), insulin should not be given to a diabetic child, etc. Such is not faith in God. It is rather presumption. It is most certainly true that Jesus Christ is the healer, and He most decidedly heals today, but it is neither sin nor lack of trust in God to take medicine or to go to the hospital.

HEALING

The Lord has healed many people while they were taking medicine, even though the medicine may or may not have done them any good. The Lord has also healed countless people in hospitals. If such showed a lack of faith, there would be no healing under these circumstances.

Actually, the Bible tells us that in the coming kingdom age, the Lord Himself will dispense medicine. The Scripture says this concerning the trees that grow beside the river, which flows out from the temple in Jerusalem: *"And the leaf thereof for medicine"* (Ezek. 47:12).

Trusting the Lord concerns a total dependence placed on Him for salvation. Nothing that man has can save, which includes the church, money, good works, etc. Therefore, total trust must be placed in Christ for salvation and for victory over sin in all its forms—not in Christ plus the church, Christ plus the psychologists, Christ plus religious leaders, etc., but Christ only!

Also, please allow me to say it one more time: Christ is the source, and the Cross is the means!

At first glance, almost all Christians would claim their total trust is in Christ. However, if they are put to the test, for many it would be quickly revealed that they are trusting in Christ plus their church or Christ plus something else, which, in reality, is no trust at all, at least as the Lord looks at it (Jas. 1:6-8).

Much of the time, total trust in God will mean separation, not only from the world, but also from institutionalized religion.

AN AGREEMENT WITH SATAN

"Hearken not to Hezekiah: for thus says the king of Assyria, Make an agreement with me by a present, and come out to me: and

eat you every one of his vine, and every one of his fig tree, and drink you every one the waters of his own cistern" (Isa. 36:16).

In other words, the war will cease if you will *"make an agreement with me."* This has ever been Satan's ploy. The fight that the true Christian faces, which seems to be never-ending, and which demands more of us than we seem to have, can come to an instant end if we will only forsake Hezekiah, i.e., Christ, and accept the offers made by Satan. However, Satan is a liar, and we should always recognize this.

We ask the reader to carefully notice that Rabshakeh's promises were great! He promised prosperity and cessation of conflict. It is a tantalizing prospect for many Christians. The riches sound good, and the absence of conflict sounds even better! In today's modern climate, many have *"deserted Hezekiah"* and opted for the promises of *"the Assyrian."*

However, the modern Christian, as then, must realize that *"his own vine"* will bring forth no fruit, and *"his own cistern"* will bring forth no living water. The True Vine is Christ. Only the branches in that True Vine will bring forth fruit.

Likewise, water drawn out of one's own cistern slakes no thirst; rather, it causes even more thirst. Only if we drink His water from His well will we never thirst again (Jn. 4:14).

LYING PROMISES

"Until I come and take you away to a land like your own land, a land of corn and wine, a land of bread and vineyards. Beware lest Hezekiah persuade you, saying, The Lord will deliver us. Has any

of the gods of the nations delivered his land out of the hand of the king of Assyria?" (Isa. 36:17-18).

Despite the golden promises, the plan was to take Judah captive into Assyria exactly as they had already taken Ephraim. This is also Satan's plan for the modern Christian! He promises everything, but only gives captivity. His terminology is amazing.

Judah was *"a land of corn and wine."* So, why would they want to leave it? Why does the modern Christian want to leave the land of corn and wine that God has given him and go instead into the captivity of Satan? Only with Christ is there freedom. All else is captivity.

The boast of Rabshakeh was not hollow, at least regarding the gods of the nations. As far as the Assyrians were concerned, this was a religious war. Their success in the religious character of their wars justified this boast. The pervading idea of the inscriptions is that wars were undertaken for glory of the Assyrian deities, particularly Asshur, for the chastisement of his enemies, with the object of establishing the laws and worship of Asshur in each country brought under subjection.

ASSHUR, THE IDOL

The nations of the world in those days fought under the protection of their own gods; thus, each war was a struggle between the Assyrian deities and those of the nation with which they were contending. Hitherto, Assyria had met with almost uniform success. Because they had easily defeated the northern kingdom of Israel, which was supposed to have the same God as Judah, they felt that surely Judah's God also would fall to Asshur.

The Assyrian king acted as regent on earth for the national god Asshur, to whom he reported his activities regularly. Thus, Assyrian campaigns were conceived, at least in part, as holy wars against those who failed to avow their sovereignty or dared to breach the borders of his land. In the event of rebellion, such campaigns were ruthlessly pursued.

Asshur's primary temple was at the capital of Asshur, with various deities thought to guard the interests of the other cities. Aneu and Adad resided at Asshur, having temples and associated ziggurats there, while Ishtar, goddess of war and love, was worshipped at Nineveh as Ishtar of Arbella. She also held sway at Erbil.

Nabu, god of wisdom and patron of the sciences, had temples at both Nineveh and Calah (Mimrud), where there were libraries collected by royal officials and housed in part in the Nabu (Nebo) temple.

Sin, the moon-god, and his priests and priestesses had a temple and a cluster at Ehulhaul in Harran and were in close association with their counterpart in Ur. It was Ur of the Chaldees from which Abraham came.

MORE AND MORE HEATHEN GODS

In general, divine consorts and less prominent deities had shrines within the major temple. Thus, at Calah, where the temples of Ninurta, god of war and hunting, Ishtar, and Nabu had been discovered, there were places for such deities as Shala, Gula, Ea, and Damkina.

In most respects, the Assyrian religion differed little from that of Babylonia from whence it had been derived. Most of the legends and myths of these gods were derived from a corruption of the Hebrew Bible. For example, they described the creation of man following a strike against the gods and also the flood. This provides a close parallel with the Old Testament from which it was, no doubt, derived.

Another example is that of Sargon of Agade, who was saved at birth by being placed in a reed basket on the river Euphrates and being rescued by a gardener who brought him to the king. This is obviously very similar to the story of baby Moses.

It is, therefore, obvious that the powers of darkness were arrayed against the power of God.

SAMARIA

"Where are the gods of Hamath and Arphad? where are the gods of Sepharvaim? and have they delivered Samaria out of my hand?" (Isa. 36:19).

In this passage, Rabshakeh boasted of his god, Asshur, over the gods of Hamath and Arphad. Sennacherib saw no distinction between the cities where Jehovah was worshipped, as supposedly in Samaria, and those that acknowledged other gods. As Samaria fell, why should not Jerusalem? He, therefore, equated Samaria's god with Judah. While it is true that Jehovah was supposed to be Samaria's god, Samaria had long ago forsaken

Jehovah for the worship of idols. This was the very reason that the northern kingdom had been destroyed and its people taken captive. This, Sennacherib did not understand!

In his thinking, the god of the nation was represented only in the fact that he was stronger or weaker. Neither Rabshakeh nor Sennacherib could imagine Jehovah dealing with His people in a positive or negative way. Paul said, *"But the natural man receives not the things of the Spirit of God: for they are foolishness unto him: neither can he know them, because they are spiritually discerned"* (I Cor. 2:14).

THE INSULTS AGAINST JEHOVAH

"Who are they among all the gods of these lands, that have delivered their land out of my hand, that the Lord should deliver Jerusalem out of my hand? But they held their peace, and answered him not a word: for the king's commandment was, saying, Answer him not. Then came Eliakim, the son of Hilkiah, who was over the household, and Shebna the scribe, and Joah, the son of Asaph, the recorder, to Hezekiah with their clothes rent, and told him the words of Rabshakeh" (Isa. 36:20-22).

In verse 20, Rabshakeh puts Jehovah in the same class as the idol gods of other nations. This means that Jehovah was ridiculed, lambasted, insulted, and slandered, even reduced to the level of man-made images.

That Jehovah would deliver Judah, of that there was no doubt! However, the manner in which He delivered them was because of this very insult. The Lord would humiliate the Assyrians so greatly that Sennacherib would not recover. Judah would not suffer the loss of one single person or even an arrow being shot against the wall of Jerusalem. So much for the god Asshur!

There are occasions when faith's most effective reply to insulting language is the dignity of silence, and her best refuge is prayer. Faith does not lend to bluster, but rather to quiet assurance in the promises of God; consequently, most of what today claims to be faith is not faith, but rather foolishness.

Upon hearing the words of Rabshakeh, these individuals named in verse 22 came to Hezekiah *"with their clothes rent."* These officials meant to mark their horror at Rabshakeh's blasphemies. Shebna the scribe was dressed in sackcloth the same as Eliakim. There, however, the similarity ended. Eliakim wanted the will of God, while Shebna wanted his place and position salvaged. Unfortunately, Shebna describes far too many modern Christians.

I give my heart to Thee,
O Jesus most desired;
And heart for heart the gift shall be,
For You my soul has fired.

You hearts alone would move,
You only hearts do love;
I would love You as You love me,
O Jesus most desired.

What offering can I make,
Dear Lord, to love like Thine;
That You, the Word, did stoop to take,
A human form like mine?

"Give Me your heart, My son,"
Lord, You my heart has won;
I would love You as You loved me,
O Jesus most desired.

Your heart is opened wide,
It's offered love most free,
That heart to heart I may abide,
And hide my self in Thee.

Ah, how Your love does burn,
Till I that love return!
I would love You as You loved me,
O Jesus most desired.

Here finds my heart its rest,
Repose that knows no shock.

The strength of love that keeps it blest,
In You, the riven Rock.

My soul, as girt around,
Her citadel has found;
I would love You as You loved me,
O Jesus most desired.

HEZEKIAH

CHAPTER 5

THUS SAITH THE LORD

THUS SAITH THE LORD

"And it came to pass, when King Hezekiah heard it, that he rent his clothes, and covered himself with sackcloth, and went into the house of the Lord" (Isa. 37:1).

HOPE IS IN THE LORD ALONE

This chapter is actually a continuation of the previous; therefore, the two constitute but one narrative.

Whatever difficulties of faithlessness plagued Hezekiah previously, they had now been thrown off, and he was doing what should be done. He was taking his difficulties to the Lord. The Assyrians here were threatening his destruction, and he realized there was no hope except in God. Someone has asked the question, "Is it possible to live so close to God that these vicissitudes of life can be avoided?"

It is certainly possible to live close enough to the Lord that some problems may be avoided, but it is not possible that all be avoided! Such is obvious in the lives of Paul, David, Abraham, and others. Irrespective of the degree of consecration, there are certain areas of self and the flesh in one's life that cannot be rectified without some degree of suffering. The Scripture says this concerning Christ: *"Though He were a Son, yet learned He obedience by the things which He suffered"* (Heb. 5:8).

OBEDIENCE

Please notice that He "learned obedience" but not "to be obedient," which is quite another thing! Had he learned to be obedient, that would imply that He had been disobedient, which He never was. Conversely, all of us at one time or another have been disobedient; therefore, God allows certain impasses to teach us to be obedient and not to be disobedient.

REPENTANCE

Hezekiah did two things when he heard this devastating news. The phrase, *"He rent his clothes, and covered himself with sackcloth,"* denotes humility and brokenness before the Lord, which are required for true repentance. It is the place and position to which none of us are easily brought! The wearing of sackcloth denoted helplessness and a proper evaluation of oneself. The sackcloth was slit in several places. This, in essence, took the place of the leper. The leper had to wear his coat torn down the back, denoting the fact that he was a leper and that he was helpless to save or cleanse himself. As stated, men, even Christian men, are not easily brought to this position; however, it was a position the Holy Spirit aspired for Hezekiah to be brought, and us as well. Such is the prerequisite for true repentance.

The wearing of sackcloth at certain times was a custom under the old law of Moses but is not the custom presently. There is no record of such in the New Testament; however, that which it represented, namely, a *"broken and contrite spirit,"* must very well be evident in the heart for the Lord to move on our behalf.

THE HOUSE OF THE LORD

The phrase, *"And went into the house of the Lord,"* refers to the temple.

Those who came to Hezekiah (Eliakim, Shebna, etc.) also wore sackcloth, but they did not go into the house of the Lord. Hezekiah did what they had done, but he went further, showing a deeper sense of need and affliction than these officials.

The temple was not only a place for offering praise and sacrifice but was also a *"house of prayer"* (I Ki. 8:28-30). Under the old economy of God, the Lord dwelt between the mercy seat and the cherubim. Now, due to the crucifixion and resurrection of Christ, the Holy Spirit dwells within our hearts, and does so on a continuing basis (Jn. 14:16; I Cor. 3:16).

THE COURT OF ISRAEL

When it says that Hezekiah *"went into the house of the Lord,"* it was referring to the court of Israel, which was sometimes referred to as the *"court of men,"* which was the nearest court to the brazen altar. Since he was not a priest, he could not go into the Holy Place, which the priests could and did in the carrying out of their daily duties.

In coming to the court of Israel, which, as stated, was the nearest to the brazen altar, he was coming, in effect, close to the Cross, where every believer must come.

The Lord cannot accept anyone, whether then or now, except he come by and through the Cross. It is the Cross of Christ that gives us access to the throne of God—the Cross alone! (Eph. 2:13-18). In other words, without what Jesus did at the Cross, which was to atone for all sin, past, present, and future— at least, for all who will believe—men would have no access at all. Everything, and without exception, is tied to the Cross (I Cor. 1:17-18, 23; 2:2)!

THE PROPHET ISAIAH

"And he sent Eliakim, who was over the household, and Shebna the scribe, and the elders of the priests covered with sackcloth, unto Isaiah the prophet the son of Amoz" (Isa. 37:2).

Some months earlier, Hezekiah had sent ambassadors to the Assyrians, seeking accommodations. They were insulted instead! Now he came to Isaiah, or rather sent certain men to Isaiah, which he should have done in the first place.

Great is the church, city, or nation that has within its confines one like Isaiah! Sadly, however, today there is little room either in the church or state for Isaiah.

A DAY OF TROUBLE

"And they said unto him, Thus says Hezekiah, This day is a day of trouble, and of rebuke, and of blasphemy: for the children are come to the birth, and there is not strength to bring forth" (Isa. 37:3).

This day of trouble, rebuke, and blasphemy means "a day of reproof and chastisement." This speaks of the insults by the Assyrians against God and Judah. Even Hezekiah himself deserved reproof for having so long placed his reliance upon Egypt, though now, apparently, he had turned to Jehovah and was relying on Him alone.

NOT ENOUGH STRENGTH TO
BRING FORTH THE BIRTH

The phrase, *"The children are come to the birth,"* was then a proverbial phrase for a time of extreme difficulty. To be sure, this was one of those times. Judah was in sore trouble and was expecting deliverance; however, it seemed now as if she would not have enough strength to go through the crisis but would perish through weakness.

Despite the previous prophecies of Isaiah, which seemingly were not given the credence they should have been given, Hezekiah now felt that the situation was very close to hopeless. What in the world could Judah do against the Assyrian monolith? The Assyrians had already taken the entirety of the balance of Judah, with only Jerusalem now remaining, and the Assyrians were now demanding surrender. What could Judah do?

THE MODERN CHURCH

Due to the present ability for mass communication, the greatest opportunity for world evangelism that has ever been known is upon us; however, there is not strength to bring forth. The children are ready to be born into the kingdom, but the modern church is too busy protecting its own turf. It is torn by infighting, trying to confess its way to riches, or going down to Egypt, i.e., the world, for help! Consequently, that which is the most important, the bringing of souls into the kingdom, which is why Christ came, is being relegated to third or fourth place, if any place at all!

The strength of which Hezekiah spoke was not military preparedness or riches concerning gold or silver, but rather the power of God. The modern church can boast of strength in many areas, such as money, numbers, education, etc., but not in that which counts the most, not in that which, in reality, counts at all. I continue to speak of the power of God.

There is only one way to get this strength, and that is the same way Hezekiah obtained it. We must, spiritually speaking, cover ourselves with *"sackcloth"* and *"go into the house of the Lord,"* i.e., come back to the Cross!

MERIT WITH GOD

"It may be the Lord your God will hear the words of Rabshakeh, whom the king of Assyria his master has sent to reproach the living God, and will reprove the words which the Lord your God has

heard: wherefore lift up your prayer for the remnant that is left" (Isa. 37:4).

Some have criticized Hezekiah's faith because he used the words *"it may be."* Quite possibly, it was a lack of faith; however, he knew that the Lord had recently allowed Samaria to be taken into captivity, and he suspected that Judah's sins were as bad as Samaria's, or possibly worse. As well, up till now, he had not personally conducted himself as he should have done toward Jehovah. This is the reason he said, *"There is not strength to bring forth"* and *"it may be."*

Notice in this verse the manner in which Hezekiah couched his terminology. He didn't plead with the Lord regarding the merit of Judah, but rather the blasphemy of Rabshakeh. He knew that neither he nor Judah had any merit with God. This attitude should be a model for us, as well.

"The remnant that is left" refers to the great number of Judae-ans who had already been taken captive from the other cities of Judah, with only those who were in Jerusalem remaining.

ISAIAH, THE PROPHET OF GOD

"So the servants of King Hezekiah came to Isaiah" (Isa. 37:5).

Presently, the modern church is facing the same problem in the spiritual sense that Hezekiah faced in that day of long ago. He went to Isaiah, the prophet of God. The modern church, sad to say, is going to the psychologists, i.e., Satan. Consequently, the church wanders as sheep with no shepherd. It doesn't know where it has been, where it is, or where it is going.

The greatest treasure the church has is those who know how to touch God. Tragically, there aren't many; more tragic still, they are little consulted, if at all!

THUS SAYS THE LORD …

"And Isaiah said unto them, Thus shall you say unto your master, Thus says the Lord, Be not afraid of the words that you have heard, wherewith the servants of the king of Assyria have blasphemed Me" (Isa. 37:6).

Isaiah immediately sent a message to Hezekiah. The message was threefold:

1. The phrase, *"Thus says the Lord,"* presents the greatest message that one could ever hear, whether positive or negative. If it is from the Lord, even if it is negative, an offer of grace and mercy will always accompany it. God's judgment is always corrective rather than punitive. The church at this hour has never been more rife with *"thus says the Lord,"* when, in reality, there has been little message from the Lord, if anything at all. Such are false prophets. Regrettably, an apostate church would rather hear a false word than a true word.

2. The phrase, *"Be not afraid of the words that you have heard,"* simply means, as it regards Rabshakeh, *"fear not."* In fact, Rabshakeh's words had brought fear to the heart of Hezekiah, and *"fear has torment."* Over 80 times in the

Bible, the Lord says, *"Fear not!"* Surely Hezekiah had known of the prophecies previously given by Isaiah that spoke of victory over the Assyrians (Isa. 31:3-9). Perhaps Hezekiah, due to his faithlessness, did not properly understand the content, or else, he was afraid that his own vacillation could have negated these promises of God. At any rate, he was afraid, or else the Lord would not have so admonished him! Fear shows a lack of love for God and produces faithlessness (I Jn. 4:18).

3. The phrase, *"Wherewith the servants of the king of Assyria have blasphemed me,"* proclaims the fact that the Lord hears every word, which should be obvious. Here we find part of the reason the Lord did what He did concerning the sending of an angel to kill 185,000 Assyrians in one night. It was because of Rabshakeh's blasphemy against Him.

As we have stated, it was not because of the merit of Hezekiah, as repentant as he was. Without fear of contradiction, I think we can say that whatever God does for us, it is never because of merit on our part. It is because of merit on His part.

THE BLAST

"Behold, I will send a blast upon him, and he shall hear a rumor, and return to his own land; and I will cause him to fall by the sword in his own land" (Isa. 37:7).

The phrase, *"I will send a blast upon him,"* rather meant, *"I will put a spirit within him,"* which actually says, "I will remove from Sennacherib the spirit of pride and arrogance and instead, will infuse into his heart a spirit of hesitation and fear."

The *"fear"* or *"blast"* refers to the Lord sending an angel, who, in one night, would kill 185,000 Assyrian soldiers. To be sure, this put a severe crimp in the plans of Sennacherib. When the Lord takes a hand in a situation, He has ample provision to enable Him to do whatever He desires, as this verse proves. No mere mortal can bring about such results; therefore, it is useless to place trust in men. Believers should seek the Lord about everything, desiring His direction, which will then garner His results.

Sennacherib did return to his own land, in defeat, we might quickly add, and some years later was murdered by two of his sons exactly as Isaiah prophesied. While Sennacherib did make forays into other parts of the world before he was murdered by his sons, to be sure, he made no effort toward Judah whatsoever, and for all the obvious reasons.

THE KING OF ETHIOPIA

"So Rabshakeh returned, and found the king of Assyria warring against Libnah: for he had heard that he was departed from Lachish. And he heard say concerning Tirhakah king of Ethiopia, He is come forth to make war with you. And when he heard it, he sent messengers to Hezekiah, saying" (Isa. 37:8-9).

After Rabshakeh concluded his mission, not realizing the wheels he had set in motion, he returned to Sennacherib, where he found him attempting to destroy Libnah. It seems that this was the next stronghold on the way to Egypt. It was, therefore, strategically logical that this city be eliminated in his eventual march in that direction.

The Holy Spirit through the prophet Isaiah now gives us some more information regarding Sennacherib.

"Tirhakah king of Ethiopia" is among the most famous of the monarchs belonging to this period. It seems this king had defeated Egypt and now ruled both Ethiopia and Egypt.

According to the Egyptian records, he had a reign of at least 26 years in Egypt—from 693 B.C. to 667 B.C. Actually, at this time, Shabatok, the deputy of *"Tirhakah,"* ruled Egypt and was now being pressed by Sennacherib. Tirhakah would go to the rescue of Shabatok. His movement provoked rather than alarmed Sennacherib, who had already defeated one Egyptian army a short time before. He was, consequently, confident of success against any effort that the Egyptians could make. Due to these recent happenings, Sennacherib sent other messengers to Hezekiah, demanding immediate surrender. If Jerusalem surrendered, then it seems Sennacherib thought he could avoid war with the Ethiopians, and do so by going back to Assyria. However, he could not leave Jerusalem unattended, or so he thought!

JEHOVAH

"Thus shall you speak to Hezekiah king of Judah, saying, Let not your God, in whom you trust, deceive you, saying, Jerusalem shall not be given into the hand of the king of Assyria" (Isa. 37:10).

More than likely, the prophecy of Isaiah concerning Jerusalem being spared had already been reported to Sennacherib. As a result, he gave his reply.

Sennacherib recognized Jehovah as a god, the god of the Jews, but put Him on the same par with the other *"gods of the nations,"* and did not believe in Him being able to contend with Asshur, the god of the Assyrians.

Sennacherib reasoned that if Hezekiah's priests or prophets were actually giving him assurance of protection and deliverance, this was only deceiving him. Ironically, this is very similar to my own personal experience, which obviously is on a much smaller scale.

In October 1991, after much effort by the powers of darkness to destroy this ministry, we made the decision to trust the Lord for His complete deliverance.

Upon making this decision, we were told that we were being deceived. In other words, these particular preachers were saying that God would not deliver—the same words, incidentally, that Sennacherib said. Sennacherib was a tool of Satan and, likewise, anyone else who claims such, i.e., *"the Lord will not deliver,"* are tools of Satan, whether they are people or preachers!

THE KINGS OF ASSYRIA

"Behold, you have heard what the kings of Assyria have done to all lands by destroying them utterly; and shall you be delivered?" (Isa. 37:11).

The kings of Assyria were, in fact, very powerful:

- Tiglath-Pileser I called himself "the conquering hero, the terror of whose name has overwhelmed all regions."

- Shalmaneser II called himself "the marcher over the whole world."

- Shamas-Bul called himself "the trampler on the world."

- Sargon said, "The gods had granted him the exercise of his sovereignty over all kings."

- Sennacherib said, "Asshur, father of the gods, among all kings firmly has raised me, and over all who dwell in the countries he calls to increase my weapons."

From the first to the last on their inscriptions, the monarchs of the Assyrian Empire claimed a universal dominion. Therefore, these boasts were not hollow threats!

THE GODS OF THE NATIONS?

"Have the gods of the nations delivered them which my fathers have destroyed, as Gozan, and Haran, and Rezeph, and the children of Eden which were in Telassar? Where is the king of Hamath, and the king of Arphad, and the king of the city of Sepharvaim, Hena, and Ivah?" (Isa. 37:12-13).

Among these areas that were conquered by the Assyrians was "*Gozan,*" which is, beyond all doubt, the region known to the Greeks as "*Gauzanitis,*" which was the eastern portion of Upper Mesopotamia. The Assyrian conquest of this tract is indicated by the settlement of the Israelites in the region that they had taken captive some years before (the northern kingdom of Israel).

Haran is the well-known city of Nahor (Gen. 24:10). Nahor was the grandfather of Abraham.

Sennacherib, like Satan, delighted in boasting of his victories. Such was done to strike fear into the hearts of his victims. The idea is, if these mighty ones fell, what can you do?

CHRIST AND THE CROSS ARE OUR STRENGTH

In the realm of Christianity, what happens to other Christians should have no bearing whatsoever on even the weakest child of God. Christ and His Cross are the strength of every individual Christian, not something or someone else! Therefore, if the stumbling of one causes the fall of another, which, to be sure, can very easily happen, still, at the same time, this is a sign that the individual had his eyes on man and not on Christ, or at least not on Christ as He should! Actually, the cause of any difficulty with sin on the part of any Christian is because of a lack of understanding regarding God's prescribed order of victory, which has been given over and over in this volume.

If proper direction is understood and maintained as it regards Christ and the Cross, whatever difficulties there might be will take care of themselves.

VICTORY OVER THE WORLD,
THE FLESH, AND THE DEVIL

The particular heading, "Victory over the world, the flesh, and the Devil," had its origin with our early church fathers. They were right in what they were saying. The world's system is a distinct enemy of the child of God, and so is the flesh. Of course, Satan also falls into that category, as certainly should be obvious!

The Lord has one method and one way of victory—not 10, not five, not even two—only one. That one way is the Cross of the Lord Jesus Christ. It is the Cross of Christ that makes everything possible.

To be sure, every single thing that our Lord now has, He has always had. However, due to the fact that the blood of bulls and goats could not take away sins, this meant that the sin debt hung over man, even the godliest, proclaiming the fact that due to this, the Lord was extremely limited as to what He could do for man. The Cross changed all of that. The Cross satisfied the sin debt, which made it possible for the Holy Spirit to come into the heart and life of the believer, and there to abide forever (Jn. 14:16).

The major problem today is that few Christians understand how the Holy Spirit works. Not understanding how He works, we are bereft of so much of what He can do for us.

THE WAY THE HOLY SPIRIT WORKS

In 1988, in the month of March, which was a disastrous time for this ministry, I did not see how we could survive, and on top of that, I knew full well that the fault was mine. But yet, even though the fault was mine, because I understood not God's prescribed order of victory and was, therefore, trying to overcome in all the wrong ways, there was very little that I could do, if anything. To be sure, there is absolutely nothing anyone else can do, no matter how consecrated or zealous for the Lord, if they do not understand God's prescribed way.

If Satan attacks a believer, and that believer doesn't understand what the Holy Spirit, through Paul, has taught us in Chapter 6 of Romans, no matter how hard that believer tries, no matter how zealous he might be, no matter how consecrated he might be, and no matter how he may seek the Lord otherwise, failure will be the inevitable result.

This is very important, so please let me say it again: The Lord has one way of victory and one way only. If we know that way, we can walk in victory! While the Bible does not teach sinless perfection, it most definitely does teach that sin is not to have dominion over us (Gal. 6:14).

If we don't know God's way, failure is the result. Regrettably, there is not one Christian out of 100,000 who does know the way. I realize that is quite a statement, but it happens to be true.

GOD'S PATTERN

The Holy Spirit works exclusively by and through the Cross of Christ. In other words, it's what Jesus did at the Cross that gives the Holy Spirit the legal means to do all that He does (Rom. 8:2).

Before the Cross, the Holy Spirit was very limited as to what He could do for mankind. For instance, He could not come into the heart and life of the believer to abide. While He did come into the hearts and lives of certain prophets and certain kings to help them carry out their tasks assigned to them, when that ended, He left. All of this was because the terrible sin debt was still upon man, even the godliest of men.

Consequently, before the Cross, when a believer passed away, such a believer did not go to heaven but was taken down into paradise. This was and is a place next door to hell, but yet, separated by a great gulf. It is there presently, but the paradise side is now empty (Lk. 16:19-31).

Once again, these believers, which included all the Old Testament saints, could not be taken to heaven when they died because the sin debt was still there and because the blood of bulls and goats, as stated, could not take away sins. While it covered sins and served as a stopgap measure, it could not take those sins away. However, when Jesus died on the Cross of Calvary, thereby, atoning for all sin, past, present, and future— at least for all who will believe (Jn. 3:16)—this made it possible for the Holy Spirit to come into the heart and life of each believer, which He does since the Cross, there to abide forever (Jn. 14:16).

So, understanding this, the believer is to place his or her faith exclusively in Christ and what Christ did for us at the Cross. This is the only faith that the Holy Spirit will honor, but sadly, this is a great truth that most in the modern church do not know.

I WILL SHOW YOU THINGS ABOUT THE
HOLY SPIRIT YOU DO NOT NOW KNOW

I wish to go back and lay a foundation for how this great truth that I've just given you came about.

It was in March 1988. The weather was beautiful and warm, and I had stayed home from the office in order to seek the Lord, which I would spend the day doing. In fact, I did this at least once a week, spending the entire day seeking God and getting direction, and this day was to prove to be a very difficult time. In fact, it was extremely difficult, but at the same time, it was a day of blessing.

While prayer is an absolute must in the life of the believer, that is, if we are to have the leading and direction of the Lord, prayer, as wonderful as it is, will not give a believer victory over the world, the flesh, and the Devil. Jesus said, *"You shall know the truth, and the truth shall make you free"* (Jn. 8:32).

I've always had a strong prayer life. In fact, such was taught to me by my grandmother. It has helped me to touch this world for Christ. At the same time, if one doesn't know the truth in particular biblical areas, a strong prayer life will not give you victory, even though it will greatly help you. That may be hard for some people to understand, but it is the truth.

As I began to pray that particular morning, after a period of time, the powers of darkness came against me in such a way as I have seldom, if ever, known. As Satan began to taunt me, he knew exactly what to say.

"You have disgraced yourself, your church, your family, and above all, the work of God. You might as well take what money you have in the bank and just disappear." (I had $800 in the bank.) The pressure grew so intense that, at one particular time, I stood near a fence at the back of our property and told the Lord, "You've got to help me. No human being can stand this."

THE GLORY OF GOD

It was only a few minutes later that it happened. One moment, the powers of darkness were so strong that I literally didn't feel that I could stand it much longer, and then, all of a sudden, it changed. It was like the Lord said, "It's enough," and Satan disappeared. As terribly bad as I had felt as the powers of darkness came against me, all of a sudden, the very opposite was true. I had never felt so wonderful in all of my life. A few moments before, it had seemed as if 500 pounds were on my shoulders, and now it seemed as though I was floating on thin air. I don't know how to explain it except with the halting words I've just given you.

Then the Lord spoke to my heart and said, "I'm going to show you some things about the Holy Spirit you do not now know." That was all that He said, but I had absolutely no doubt that it was the Lord.

Of course, the Holy Spirit is God, and as such, there are all kinds of things about Him that we do not know. However, the Lord was addressing the petition I had been making before Him as it regarded victorious Christian living.

I knew the Lord had spoken to me, but yet, there was nothing else that was forthcoming. What did He actually mean?

That was 1988. It was not until 1997, nine years later, that the Lord fulfilled that promise.

THE SIN NATURE

For nine years I sought the Lord earnestly, especially from the years 1991 to 1997. In fact, during those years, we had two prayer meetings every day. Even though the Lord greatly blessed, still, there was no definitive answer. Actually, I didn't even really know that for which I was asking, only that I was missing something.

I don't really remember the month, but it was in 1997. The Lord first of all opened up to me the meaning of the sin nature, taking me straight to the Word of God, which on this occasion was Romans, Chapter 6. The sin nature, the Lord told me, was the problem, and more so, that I did not understand how it should be handled. At that time, the Lord did not relate to me at all what the solution was, only what the problem was.

In all of my years of living for God, I had never heard one single sermon on the sin nature. I had never read one message on the sin nature. I had never heard a preacher say anything about the sin nature. I had read the word a few times, but that was about it.

THE CROSS

But pure and simple, the Lord wondrously explained to me exactly what it was, how it functioned, and how it was not to function. Actually, He used a book written by Kenneth Wuest, one of the great Greek scholars of the 20TH century. While studying Chapter 6 of Romans, I happened to pick up his book on Romans to see what he had to say about a particular passage. As I began to read, the Holy Spirit began to open it up to me, showing me exactly what the sin nature is.

However, as just stated, He did not give me the solution to the problem, only what the problem was. That was to come a few days later.

At any rate, I remember walking the floor of my office with tears rolling down my face. Now I knew the cause of failure. It's a terrible thing to struggle with all of one's strength and power and still fail anyway. But yet, that is happening millions of times over, each and every day, simply because believers do not understand this biblical doctrine of the sin nature and how it is to be opposed.

That early morning hour, I knew that I now had the answer as to the cause, but, as stated, I did not know the cure. That came about a few days later.

It was in one of the morning prayer meetings. The Lord began to move upon my heart that morning, and this is what He said to me, which came actually in three short sentences:

1. The answer for which you seek is found in the Cross.

2. The solution for which you seek is found in the Cross.

3. The answer for which you seek is found only in the Cross.

THE HOLY SPIRIT

I knew the Lord had spoken to me, and I knew that He had given me the solution to the sin nature, which is the Cross. The question that still lingered in my mind was, "How does the Holy Spirit fit into all of this?"

In prayer the next few days, I implored the Lord about this particular question. He told me plainly that the Cross was the solution; the Cross was the answer. I knew the Holy Spirit had to play a great part in all of this, but I did not know exactly how.

The answer to that came just a few days later on our morning radio program, *A Study in the Word,* which airs over the SonLife Network owned by the ministry. (It has now been shortened to 30 minutes and airs twice a day over the network.)

Something happened at the end of the program that day that was totally unlike anything I had ever experienced. There was no one on the program except Loren Larson and me. It was coming down to the end of the program, and I opened my mouth, and something came out that I did not understand. Please believe me, I didn't understand it at all. I stated, "The Holy Spirit works exclusively within the parameters of the finished work of Christ and will not work any other way."

I had not read such a statement. Such a thought had never come to my mind. I had never heard such uttered in all of my life. It came as such a shock that I sat there speechless for a few moments. Where did I get that?

"The Holy Spirit works exclusively by and through the Cross of Christ and will not work in any other fashion."

About that time, Loren spoke up and said, "Can you give me Scripture for that?"

How could I give him Scripture when I had never heard the statement in all of my life? Of course, he did not know that. I sat there for a few moments, not knowing what to say, when I looked down at my Bible, and it was open to Romans 8:2, which said: *"The law of the Spirit of life in Christ Jesus has made me free from the law of sin and death"* (Rom. 8:2).

Instantly, I knew this was the answer to how the Holy Spirit works.

About that time, the program ended. I stood up to walk out the door when the Spirit of God came over me again. The Lord said to me, "Do you remember back in 1988 how that I said to you that I would show you things about the Holy Spirit you did not then know?" Of course, I remembered. He then said to me, "I have just kept my promise to you."

That was only the beginning. From then until now, I have continued to learn more and more about how the Holy Spirit works. However, this is the great problem in the modern church. It simply doesn't know how the Holy Spirit works.

The non-Pentecostal church, whatever it might be, simply ignores the Holy Spirit. They know precious little about Him, with the fact being that He operates almost not at all in those circles. As it regards Pentecostals, who claim to know, about all that is known is speaking with other tongues and one or more gifts of the Spirit that are occasionally used. Thank God for those gifts, and thank God on both cases for speaking with other tongues, which I do daily. However, that's about all that

Pentecostals know. They really do not know how the Holy Spirit works, and that means that virtually all in that category live a life of spiritual defeat.

So, the entire scenario that the Lord revealed to me could be summed up in the following:

- Jesus Christ is the source of all things we receive from God.

- The Cross of Christ is the means by which all of this is done.

- Our faith must rest exclusively in Christ and the Cross, which is actually the story of the Bible.

- With that being done, the Holy Spirit will then grandly work, and work powerfully on our behalf.

THE METHODS OF SATAN

"And Hezekiah received the letter from the hand of the messengers, and read it: and Hezekiah went up unto the house of the Lord, and spread it before the Lord" (Isa. 37:14).

This last message was sent to Hezekiah from Sennacherib in a letter. In II Chronicles 32:17, the word *letters* is used, signifying plurality and indicating an arrogant, insulting, and boastful correspondence. In Isaiah 39:1, we will find that Hezekiah would be sent letters, as well, from the king of Babylon. As the first was insulting, these future letters would be flattering. While the two letters had nothing to do with each other, still, both were inspired by Satan. The effect of the first was to send Hezekiah to the Lord; the effect of the second was to draw him away from the Lord. Satan is more to be watched against as a polite sympathizer than as a roaring lion.

When Hezekiah received the letter from Sennacherib, he went *"unto the house of the Lord."* This is where all the problems should take the believer. The spreading of the letter *"before the Lord"* by Hezekiah did not imply that God did not know its contents previously. Rather, this was designed so that Sennacherib's reproach of the God of Judah would be ever before the Lord.

PRAYER

"And Hezekiah prayed unto the Lord, saying" (Isa. 37:15).

Every child of God has the same access presently that Hezekiah did, and even greater, due to the fact that we now function under the new covenant, which is a better covenant based on better promises (Heb. 8:6).

Prayer should be a constant with all Christians. Paul said, *"Pray without ceasing"* (I Thess. 5:17). This does not mean to be on one's knees without ceasing, but rather to be in a state of prayer constantly. Regrettably, prayer is so foreign to most Christians that when difficulties come, they are little prepared to cope spiritually. The Christian who does not know how to pray is a Christian who, by and large, has cut himself off from all help from God. Very little help, like Isaiah had, is given to anyone who does not pray unto the Lord.

PRAYER SHOULD BE CONDUCTED ON A REGULAR BASIS

If possible, every believer should have a set time each day that he gets alone with the Lord for a short period of time, and for all the obvious reasons. In fact, without a perpetual prayer life, it's impossible to have a proper relationship with the Lord. This is not meaning to imply that one can earn something from God with such a prayer life, but strictly that we can attend to business in prayer, which is actually the only way it can be conducted, at least properly. Of course, I'm speaking of business with the Lord, of which every single believer should be engaged.

When I was just a child, my grandmother taught me to pray. She taught me to believe God, and she taught me to intercede before the Lord. I can still hear one of her favorite sayings: "Jimmy, God is a big God, so ask big!" I've never forgotten that. It has helped me to touch this world for Christ.

Personally, I have always had a strong prayer life. I do so unto this hour. I come to the office each morning at about 6 a.m. Our morning television program, *The Message Of The Cross,* begins at 7 a.m. I spend at least 20 minutes with the Lord every single morning, and then, when I go home at night, I spend another 20 minutes or so with the Lord. I have to have His leading and guidance in all that I do, and this can only be ascertained by having a proper prayer life.

If every believer would do somewhat that which I have suggested, they would find an improvement in their lifestyles to such a degree as to defy all description. Unfortunately, most modern believers have little or no prayer life at all. Consequently, they have no leading or guidance by the Holy Spirit at all. That is tragic, especially considering that the Lord, with His almighty power and all consummate knowledge and wisdom, is always available.

HOW TO PRAY!

When the believer goes before the Lord, he should make it a habit, first of all, to go before Him with thanksgiving and praise. The psalmist said: *"Enter into His gates with thanksgiving, and into His courts with praise: be thankful unto Him, and bless His name"* (Ps. 100:4).

Of course, as is obvious, the psalmist was speaking of the gates and courts that led into the temple. First of all, the Israelite was to enter into the gate of the temple with thanksgiving; then he was to go into the courts of the Lord with praise.

Due to the new covenant, there is no longer an earthly temple where we are to worship the Lord. So, it could be said, that we are now privileged to first of all enter into His presence (gates) with thanksgiving, and then, into His throne (courts) with praise. This simply means that when going to prayer, the believer should not immediately begin petitioning the Lord for certain things. Rather, he should thank Him first of all, for all the good things that He is presently doing for us.

PRAISE AND WORSHIP

To be blunt, this shows good manners. We are then to take our petitions to the Lord, that is, whatever it is we need (Lk. 11:5-13).

We will also find that as the Spirit of God draws us into the Lord's presence, praise will make up a great part of our seeking the Lord (Ps. 150). Admittedly, prayer is hard work, and it's harder still because Satan will do everything within his power to keep us from praying. However, prayer is where leading and direction are given. In fact, as stated, without a proper prayer life, there can be precious little relationship with the Lord, precious little leading of the Holy Spirit, and precious few victories won, if any!

O LORD OF HOSTS

"O Lord of Hosts, God of Israel, who dwells between the cherubims, You are the God, even You alone, of all the kingdoms of the earth: You have made heaven and earth" (Isa. 37:16).

Hezekiah's prayer is very interesting and well worth our attention. It would be the same that we would pray today, with one exception. Now, we are admonished to pray to our heavenly Father in the name of Jesus (Jn. 16:23).

The phrase, *"O Lord of Hosts,"* refers to the Lord as being in charge of the great angelic host, which is so vast as to defy description. As is obvious, this vast host is at the command of the Lord.

In fact, nothing can stand against this army, or host. This tells us that the Lord has innumerable and all-sufficient resources on His side. In fact, in answer to the prayer of Hezekiah, the Lord would send just one of these untold numbers of angels, who would wreak havoc on the Assyrians. In fact, the power of the Lord is omnipotent, meaning almighty. So, we should understand that when we go to the Lord, we are going to someone who is able to do all things.

UNBELIEF

So, why is it that most Christians don't take full advantage of this of which I speak? The answer would have to be, at least for the most part, unbelief. In other words, despite being Christians, they simply do not believe the Lord. So, here we have an oxymoron—we have unbelieving believers! If believers really and truly believed the Lord—that He will answer prayer, that He stands ready to answer prayer, that He desires to answer prayer, and, therefore, that He desires that His people readily come before Him—then I think it would be obvious that believers would readily seek the face of the Lord. They don't do so simply because of unbelief.

GOD OF ISRAEL

This was saying that Jehovah is the *"God of Israel"* and is not like the gods of the other nations. However, there was no other god in Israel but Jehovah.

In a sense, this was putting God on notice. It was, in effect, an appeal unto the Lord that He would put down all other competing adversaries.

In fact, Israel was the only nation in the world of that particular time that was monotheistic, meaning that they worshipped only one God, Jehovah. All the other nations in the world were polytheistic, meaning they worshipped many gods, i.e., demon spirits.

In fact, these other so-called deities were not gods at all, but only figments of someone's imagination, actually, as stated, inspired by demon spirits. Unfortunately, this problem did not die with the ancient world. It is still very much with us presently. For instance, the Catholics look at the pope as god. They put Mary in the same category. Mormons think of Joseph Smith in the same capacity, with Muslims thinking such of Muhammad.

SPIRITUAL ADULTERY

In fact, those who claim to be in true Christendom must be very careful that they do not put their church or denomination in the place of God. Christ is the head of the church because He alone paid the price for the church by giving His life. No one or no thing is to usurp authority over that headship (Col. 1:13-20).

Paul warned against this in the first four verses of Chapter 7 of Romans. He pictured a woman married to a man, who then also takes another man for her husband. He said, *"She shall be called an adulteress."* He then went on to say that we believers are married to Christ; consequently, He can meet our every need, whatever that need might be. Tragically, most Christians look outside of Christ, such as to their church, to good works, etc. This puts them in the category of committing spiritual adultery, which means being unfaithful to Christ. It's like a man being unfaithful to his wife, or his wife being unfaithful to him.

The believer must look exclusively to Christ and what Christ did for us at the Cross, there placing his faith, and there maintaining his faith. This will then guarantee the help of the Holy Spirit, with all things provided that we need. In fact, that is the only way that provision can be made (Rom. 6:1-14; 8:1-11).

WHO DWELLS BETWEEN THE CHERUBIMS

At that time, the Lord dwelt between the mercy seat and the cherubims in the Holy of Holies; consequently, to properly worship Him, an individual had to come from wherever he might be to Jerusalem, and then to the temple. There and there only was he to offer up his sacrifice.

Now, the Lord no longer dwells in a house made with hands, but rather dwells in our hearts (I Cor. 3:16). Therefore, He can now be worshipped any time and at any place. That is partly the reason that the second covenant of grace, which is based on better promises, is greater than the first covenant (Heb. 8:6).

YOU ARE THE GOD

The phrase, *"You are the God, even You alone, of all the kingdoms of the earth,"* proclaims the fact, and in no uncertain terms, that there is no other god. Jehovah alone is God! All the gods worshipped by the other nations of the world were actually no gods at all but the manufacture of men's hands. In fact, the world has ever been trying to manufacture another god, while the church has ever been busy trying to manufacture another sacrifice.

Hezekiah was saying that there is only one God in the world. He is Jehovah, despite the claims of the heathen; furthermore, Jehovah controls *"the kingdoms of the earth."* Consequently, he was in control, not only in Judah, but in Assyria as well. Even though Sennacherib did not recognize Him as such, this did not alter the fact at all, even as Sennacherib would soon see.

THE CREATOR

The phrase, *"You have made heaven and earth,"* proclaims the Lord as creator of all things, even heaven and earth, which means, at the same time, that He controls all the kingdoms of the earth.

It is tragic that the children in our modern public school systems are taught the mindless drivel of evolution. An even greater tragedy is that many Christians, even so-called Christian leaders, now believe in a form of evolution. They claim that even though God created the heavens and the earth, still, He used the evolutionary process to do so. Such does not show broad-mindedness, but rather biblical, spiritual, and, as well, scientific ignorance. Either the Genesis account of creation is accurate, or it is not! Every true scientific evidence proves the Genesis account down to the minutest detail. If it is believed that man gradually progressed from animals over a period of many millions, or even billions, of years, then God is placed in the position of being of no greater import than a beast, for God said, *"Let Us make man in Our image, after Our likeness"* (Gen. 1:26).

Therefore, I would seriously doubt the salvation of those who call themselves Christians, who accept any part of the evolutionary lie. Those who believe the evolutionary process claim that the believers of the Genesis account of creation only have faith but no scientific proof. Actually, the opposite is true! It takes far more faith to believe in evolution than it does to believe in the Genesis account of creation.

THE WORD OF GOD

"Incline Your ear, O Lord, and hear; open Your eyes, O Lord, and see: and hear all the words of Sennacherib, which has sent to reproach the living God" (Isa. 37:17).

This is a conscious pleading of the promise made to Solomon (II Chron. 7:15). Hezekiah is calling to account this promise, as we can also call to account the many promises made in the Word of God (Mk. 9:23; Mat. 18:18; Jn. 14:14, 15:7).

Petition that is offered to the Lord without being based on the Word of God is, for the most part, a fruitless petition. All petitions should be based on the Word. They will then get guaranteed results, providing that we ask in faith and that what we are asking is *"according to His will"* (I Jn. 5:13-15).

Hezekiah wanted to impress upon the Lord the fact that Sennacherib had greatly reproached the person of the living God. Of course, the Lord knew this, even as He knows all things; however, Hezekiah felt that the Lord should take action regarding this thing, and he was right in petitioning the Lord accordingly.

ASSYRIA

"Of a truth, Lord, the kings of Assyria have laid waste all the nations, and their countries. And have cast their gods into the fire: for they were no gods but the work of men's hands, wood and stone: therefore they have destroyed them" (Isa. 37:18-19).

Actually, this was fact that was impossible to deny. For some 200 years, Assyria had pursued a career of conquests, reducing the nations that were her neighbors almost without exception. Her progress toward the west alone was marked in Scripture since there alone she came in contact with God's people. Under Pul (about 760 B.C.), she attacked Samaria (II Ki. 15:19); under Tiglath-pileser II, she carried off a portion of the Ten Tribes of Samaria, which was Israel (II Ki. 15:29). Now, she was bent on subduing Judah and so preparing the way for the reduction of Egypt. Humanly speaking, it was most unlikely that this small and weak state of Judah would be able to resist her. However, God is all-powerful and was as pleased to cast down as He had been pleased to exalt; hence, Hezekiah's appeal.

Hezekiah did not deny the existence or even the power of the Assyrians. Because of this, he would have been drummed out of the many modern so-called faith churches because they would maintain he had no faith.

THE ERRONEOUS MODERN
CONFESSION PRINCIPLE

Providing we do not dwell on the problems, it does not show a lack of faith to confess the existence of them. However, to deny the problems does not make them any less real.

I remember some years ago talking to someone over the phone who obviously was suffering with a cold. After a moment or two, I made mention of the fact that he had a cold. Instantly, he retorted, "No, I do not have a cold. I've never felt better." He had been taught, erroneously we might quickly add, that to admit any type of sickness was evidence of faithlessness. He, therefore, denied it!

Telling the truth is never a liability with God. The Lord in His Word never denies the problem but always confesses victory over the problem.

The more valuable of the fallen idols were usually carried off by the Assyrians and placed in the shrines of their own gods as trophies of victory. No doubt, great numbers of the inferior idols, i.e., those which were of wood and not even coated with metal, were burnt. Hezekiah would use the words, *"no gods."* Isaiah's favorite word for *"idols"* was *"Elilim,"* which actually means *"not gods."*

The absurdity of men worshipping these gods, which had been made by their own hands, was ever-increasingly ridiculed by the Jews, even as it should have been. In today's modern climate, to seek the help of psychologists or worldly counselors is the same as the heathen seeking their idols, and it should be ridiculed as such!

THE GLORY OF GOD

"Now therefore, O Lord our God, save us from his hand, that all the kingdoms of the earth may know that you are the Lord, even You only" (Isa. 37:20).

Hezekiah said, *"Save us ... That all the kingdoms may know."* As Hezekiah did, our every petition that is made to the Lord should not be for deliverance or triumph over enemies for our own sake or the sake of others, but rather for the glory of God.

Many prayers are not answered because they are selfish prayers. Only our wants and desires are recognized, and God's glory is too often ignored. David would have his foes consumed in order that they might know that *"God rules in Jacob unto the ends of the earth"* (Ps. 59:13), and also, in order *"that men may know that You, whose name alone is Jehovah, are the Most High over all the earth"* (Ps. 83:18). It has been well said that *"the object of all the judgments which the true prophet desires is to bring all nations into subjection to God."*

THE PROMISES OF GOD

"Then Isaiah the son of Amoz sent unto Hezekiah, saying, Thus says the Lord God of Israel, Whereas you have prayed to Me against Sennacherib king of Assyria" (Isa. 37:21).

Either Isaiah knew that Hezekiah was seeking the Lord concerning the Assyrian threat, or else the Lord revealed it to him.

Isaiah had previously prophesied what Sennacherib would do and that the Lord would deliver from his hand. The Lord had already spoken through the prophet that this heathen monarch would not be successful in his effort regarding Judah (Isa. 37:7). So, it would seem that Hezekiah was showing a lack of faith by continuing to plead when the promise had already been given. However, that is not necessarily so. First of all, the Lord wanted the faith of Hezekiah to rise to the task. Isaiah knew what the Lord would do, but, seemingly, up to this time, Hezekiah had been somewhat, if not very much, doubtful. So, there were issues to work out in Hezekiah's own heart, which could only be brought to the fore by him personally going before the Lord.

REASSURING

It also seems that frail mortals, despite the many promises of God, constantly need reassuring and reaffirmation. There are reasons for this. The victories of yesterday will not actually suffice for today. There must be fresh victories, fresh anointings, and fresh revelations from the Lord, even a repetition of what He has already given. Sadly, even in the strongest Christians, our faith is so weak that it must be constantly reassured and reinforced. Hence, David would repeatedly cry to the Lord for reassurance, despite the fact that the Lord had said that He would be king of Israel (I Sam. 16:1, 12-13; Ps. 13).

The Lord uses everything as training tools for us. Our faith is never as strong as we think it is. Our consecration also falls into the same category. To be sure, as long as our petitions are not prayers of unfaithfulness, the Lord delights in our coming before Him. He delights in reassuring us and reaffirming to us that which He has already promised. This strengthens us in His Word, and there is nothing more valuable than that.

THE ANSWER OF THE LORD

"This is the word which the Lord has spoken concerning him; The virgin, the daughter of Zion, has despised you, and laughed you to scorn; the daughter of Jerusalem has shaken her head at you" (Isa. 37:22).

The expression, "virgin daughter," represents Jerusalem as a tender maiden, weak and delicate, yet, still bold enough to stand up against Sennacherib, the mightiest monarch on the face of the earth, along with all his hosts, and bid him defiance.

Confident that the Lord would protect her, she laughed him to scorn. The phrase also has the meaning of pursuing with scornful gestures as he retreated before her, shaking her head at him in a gesture of scorn. We too should laugh at Satan's threats.

This is God's answer to the boasts of Sennacherib, and, due to its source, it must be taken extremely seriously. What Sennacherib did not know or understand was that his boasts of destruction for Jerusalem were concerned with far more than just a city. This was, first of all, the place where God dwelt. The Lord also had made promises to David, and Sennacherib's boast had come up against these promises. Of all the cities in the world of that day, this was the last one that he should have threatened!

At the same time, nearly 800 years later, the Lord would see to it that Jerusalem was completely destroyed because she would rebel against His Son, her Saviour, the Lord Jesus Christ. The rule of this episode is that men should ascertain what God is doing and do the same thing themselves. Any other direction, irrespective of its seeming strength, will come to naught.

FIGHTING AGAINST GOD

"Whom have you reproached and blasphemed? and against Whom have you exalted your voice, and lifted up your eyes on high? even against the Holy One of Israel" (Isa. 37:23).

The phrase, *"the Holy One of Israel,"* is used by Isaiah some 28 times. It is used only five other times in all the balance of Scripture.

This passage is further proof that Sennacherib was fighting not only against Jerusalem, Isaiah, and Hezekiah, but most of all, against God. As such, it was impossible for him to win. This was not only the problem of the heathen, but also even of God's children. The church too often finds itself in total opposition to the will of God. No matter how rich and powerful the denomination may be, their spiritual destruction is imminent.

THE NAZARENE CHURCH

The Nazarene Church, for instance, was begun by an evangelist greatly used of God. His name was "Uncle Bud" Robinson. In its earlier years, God blessed this church mightily. Many lives were changed; many souls were saved!

At the turn of the 20TH century when the mighty outpouring of the Holy Spirit came, which was accompanied by the speaking with other tongues, the Nazarene Church had to make a decision. It is said that at one of their yearly gatherings, after much discussion, the decision was made that anyone in their ranks who claimed to be baptized with the Holy Spirit with the evidence of speaking with other tongues, would be unceremoniously drummed out of the organization. It is also said that when the vote was cast and the decision given, a white dove, which was flying around inside the large tabernacle, flew out an open window.

Quite possibly, the happening was mere coincidence, but quite possibly, it wasn't. At any rate, since that time (the 1940s), the Nazarene Church, as a whole, has ceased to be spiritually effective. It was once led by the Holy Spirit, but now it is led by men.

The same can be said for the Assemblies of God and the Church of God, the two largest Pentecostal groups. They were once used mightily of God, but, little by little, they are denying the work and operation of the Holy Spirit. They are, little by little, no longer God-led, but rather, they are man-led.

To fight against God, no matter how much one has previously been used by the Lord, will result every time in spiritual wreckage.

REPROACHING THE LORD

"By your servants have you reproached the Lord, and have said, By the multitude of my chariots am I come up to the height of the

mountains, to the sides of Lebanon; and I will cut down the tall cedars thereof, and the choice fir trees thereof: and I will enter into the height of his border, and the forest of his Carmel" (Isa. 37:24).

In this passage, the Holy Spirit is not claiming that Sennacherib has actually uttered these words with his mouth, but that he has thought them within his heart. He has regarded the multitude of his chariots as irresistible.

The Assyrians also considered natural obstacles, by which certain nations felt protected, to be no deterrent to their advance. Neither the mountains nor the forests were considered to be a hindrance. They would scale the mountains as they had done many times and cut down the trees and ship the timber to Assyria. The thoughts of his heart were that he would occupy the whole land.

The *"forest of his Carmel,"* actually means the *"forest of his pleasure-garden."* This referred to the rich plantation tracts, covered with vines, olives, and fig trees, which formed the special glory of Judaea.

THE GREATNESS OF JEHOVAH

"I have dug, and drunk water; and with the sole of my feet have I dried up all the rivers of the besieged places. Have you not heard long ago, how I have done it; and of ancient times, that I have formed it? now have I brought it to pass, that you should be to lay waste defenced cities into ruinous heaps" (Isa. 37:25-26).

The boasting of Sennacherib in this verse declares that in the waterless deserts, he supplied his vast armies with water.

At the same time, he announced his intention and ability to dry up the mighty Nile River.

In this passage, after speaking as the person of Sennacherib, without indication, Isaiah breaks off and returns to speaking as the person of Jehovah.

Also in this passage, Sennacherib is reproached by the Holy Spirit for not knowing what he ought to have known and might have known if he had only listened to the voice of conscience and reason.

BY GOD'S PERMISSION

The words, *"Now have I brought it to pass,"* refer to the fact that all that Sennacherib had done, he had done as God's instrument, by God's permission—even by His aid at times. He had been the ax in the hand of the hewer, the saw, the rod, the staff of God's indignation, and the executor of His vengeance. He was used of God to *"lay waste defenced cities into ruinous heaps."* These cities were ordered for destruction because of their great sin and refusal to repent.

Sennacherib, however, was so lifted up in his own pride that he thought his victories were due to his own ability, tactical designs, and military expertise. Not only did Sennacherib feel this way, but from the beginning of the ages even unto modern days, man thinks in the same vein.

While it certainly is true that America should maintain a proper military defense force, still, her true source of victory is God—a source that she, sadly, little knows!

IGNORANCE IS NO EXCUSE

The first words, *"Have you not heard long ago,"* refer to the fact that ignorance is no excuse. America, for instance, is filled with Bibles. The same is true for Canada and many other countries of the world—Bibles, which for the most part, are unread!

Likewise, there is no excuse for the Muslim countries. A careful investigation will show them the fallacy of their claims. Jesus very plainly said, *"Salvation is of the Jews"* (Jn. 4:22), meaning that the seed came through Abraham to Isaac and, ultimately, through David (Mat. 1:1).

There is no reason for the Muslims not to know that. Many of the stories and illustrations in the Koran are borrowed from the much earlier Old Testament and then corrupted to suit their own fancy. They are deceived, but they are willfully deceived. Actually, the entirety of the world, at least for the most part, has heard, and not just in the recent past, but long ago, even as far back as ancient times.

Paul said, *"Because that which may be known of God is manifest in them; for God has showed it unto them. For the invisible things of Him from the creation of the world are clearly seen, being understood* (introduced) *by the things that are made, even His eternal power and Godhead; so that they are without excuse"* (Rom. 1:19-20).

SMALL POWER

"Therefore their inhabitants were of small power, they were dismayed and confounded: they were as the grass of the field, and as

the green herb, as the grass on the housetops, and as corn blasted before it be grown up. But I know your abode, and your going out, and your coming in, and your rage against Me" (Isa. 37:27-28).

God, having decreed the success of the Assyrians, affected them (in part) by infusing weakness into the nations that were adversaries. The strength of these nations destroyed by Sennacherib was reduced to the power of *"the grass of the field."* The analogy is adequately drawn by the Holy Spirit!

Sennacherib thought it was his military prowess that effected his victories when God now says the opposite. Very few in history have been different from Sennacherib!

While the Lord did give a commission to Sennacherib to chasten Judah, it was not His intention that this tiny nation be destroyed. So, the same Jehovah who had once helped Sennacherib, despite the fact that this heathen monarch knew Him not at all, now turned against Him, which would prove to have devastating results. The Lord knew his going out, his coming in, and even the thoughts of his evil heart, which were in opposition to the will of God.

THE UNWITTING INSTRUMENT

Sennacherib, even though an unwitting instrument in the hands of God, still could have known all he needed to know about God if he only had taken the time and the trouble to learn. Verse 25 says so! So, for not taking the time to learn about God, who held the key to understanding the secrets of his victories, he would incur the wrath of God.

Such speaks to all of mankind. Men make large sums of money, but they never stop to think that it is God who gives them the wisdom and ability to do so. They credit their own wisdom and knowledge when, in reality, it is God who has given the increase.

Nations become strong, but instead of using their resources to help people and to further the Word of God, they do the very opposite. They do not stop to realize that it is God who has given them the ability to prosper.

This monarch, Sennacherib, never dreamed that the One against whom he was raging was the Lord of glory, who had, in fact, given him the power to do all that he had done.

THE MEASURE WE METE

"Because your rage against Me, and your tumult, is come up into My ears, therefore will I put My hook in your nose, and My bridle in your lips, and I will turn you back by the way by which you came" (Isa. 37:29).

Sennacherib proposed the shocking cruelty of this verse for Hezekiah and his people, but, figuratively, he was made to suffer it himself. The Assyrians were in the habit of passing hooks or rings through the noses or lips of their more distinguished prisoners, and then attaching a thong to the hook or ring, by which they led the prisoners into the royal presence. At times, the heathen monarch would put out the eyes of these prisoners with the red-hot point of a spear.

The expression used in this passage derives its force from these practices, but in the present place, it is not to be understood literally.

God turned Sennacherib back and reconducted him to Nineveh, not with an actual hook or thong, but by the bridle of necessity.

THE SIGN

"And this shall be a sign unto you, You shall eat this year such as grows of itself; and the second year that which springs of the same: and in the third year sow you, and reap, and plant vineyards, and eat the fruit thereof" (Isa. 37:30).

The Lord through the prophet ceased to address Sennacherib, and now addressed Hezekiah and the totality of Judah. This verse could be translated thusly: "You did eat last year such as grew of itself, and the second year that which sprang up of the same, but in the third year, which is to come, so shall you sow, reap, and plant vineyards and eat the fruit thereof."

Agriculture had been impossible for the two prior years because of the invasion of the Assyrians. However, now God encouraged the remnant of His people to go out of the city into the country and till the ground, for He promised that the Assyrian king should never return to injure them. The entirety of Judah, which was totally controlled by the Assyrians, with the exception of Jerusalem, was to do the same. Therefore, it seems that the acute danger lasted for about two years.

THE REMNANT

"And the remnant that is escaped of the house of Judah shall again take root downward, and bear fruit upward" (Isa. 37:31).

It seems that the Assyrians in their excursion into Judah had completely depopulated the country districts. A great number had, no doubt, been killed, and more than 200,000 had been carried into captivity, with a portion having found refuge in Jerusalem.

When God sent an angel to kill 185,000 Assyrians, they then began the withdrawal. The Jews then went forth to reoccupy their lands and rebuild their towns and villages. The blessing of God was upon them. In a short time, Judah recovered her ancient vigor so that under Josiah, she was able to extend her dominion over almost the whole of the old Israelite territory (II Chron. 34:6, 18).

THE ZEAL OF THE LORD OF HOSTS

"For out of Jerusalem shall go forth a remnant, and they who escape out of Mount Zion: the zeal of the Lord of Hosts shall do this" (Isa. 37:32).

The remnant speaks of those who escaped the incursion of the last two years. As stated, many had been killed or taken captive.

The phrase, *"The zeal of the Lord of Hosts,"* is used by the Holy Spirit to ensure the fulfillment of what had been promised. God's people would be blessed and grow strong once again.

Also, this speaks of the coming glad day after the incursion of the Antichrist when the blessing of the Lord will be upon the remnant that shall escape, who once again will grow into a mighty and glorious nation and people. The total fulfillment of this passage awaits the coming kingdom age.

Satan's efforts, through the agency of the Antichrist, have been promised certain failure in these passages. The Jews will not be destroyed and will once again become a great people. The *"zeal of the Lord of Hosts"* has promised this!

CONCERNING THE KING OF ASSYRIA

"Therefore thus says the Lord concerning the king of Assyria, He shall not come into this city, nor shoot an arrow there, nor come before it with shields, nor cast a bank against it" (Isa. 37:33).

As stated, Sennacherib had conquered all of Judah, actually occupying the land, with the exception of the city of Jerusalem. He never brought an army to the walls of Jerusalem but definitely was planning to do so when he was stopped by the Lord.

All along, he had planned to lay siege against Jerusalem. The Holy Spirit, through Isaiah, now said that no siege would be laid against the city; furthermore, he would not even shoot an arrow there. All his plans for the siege would be totally and utterly foiled without even a skirmish being fought. In other words, his defeat would be utterly humiliating.

I WILL DEFEND THIS CITY

"By the way that he came, by the same shall he return, and shall not come into this city, says the Lord. For I will defend this city to save it for My own sake, and for My servant David's sake" (Isa. 37:34-35).

The declaration, *"By the way that he came, by the same shall he return,"* was the most comforting that Hezekiah could possibly receive. It assured him that he would not even be confronted by his enemy. What a mighty God we serve!

Hezekiah was told here, and by no less than the Holy Spirit through the prophet Isaiah, that he could not boast that the beauty or fervor of his prayer purchased the victory, for God told him that He would deliver the city, not for Hezekiah's sake, but for David's sake, i.e., for the Messiah's sake. In fact, everything the Lord does for us is because of the Lord Jesus Christ and what He has done for us at the Cross.

The phrase, *"I will defend his city,"* literally means, "I will cover over this city as a bird covers its young with its wings."

No doubt, Hezekiah wondered just how the Lord would bring this to pass. In the natural, such did not seem possible; in fact, it was not possible! However, whereas man is limited, God is not limited as to what He can do, that is, if we do not limit Him with a lack of faith.

THE MIRACLE

"Then the angel of the Lord went forth, and smote in the camp of the Assyrians a hundred and fourscore and five thousand: and when they arose early in the morning, behold, they were all dead corpses" (Isa. 37:36).

The word of Isaiah had its accomplishment within a few hours. At the camp of the Assyrians, wherever it was—whether at Libnah, Pelusim, or between the two—the destroying angel swooped down in the dead of night and silently, without disturbance, took the lives of 185,000 men. The camp, no doubt, was that which Sennacherib commanded.

The phrase, *"When they arose early in the morning,"* refers to the arising of the Israelites, not the Assyrians. The scene of the account was probably about 25 miles from Jerusalem. Word would have come quickly to Jerusalem concerning the dead bodies that were lying everywhere. No doubt, the bulk of Sennacherib's army numbered more than 185,000. Those who were slain were probably the officers' corps, the chariot drivers, and perhaps some regular soldiers.

The great miracle instituted by the Lord ranks in the same category as the opening of the Red Sea and the destruction of the Egyptian army, or the opening of the Jordan River and the falling of the walls of Jericho!

SENNACHERIB

"So Sennacherib king of Assyria departed, and went and returned, and dwelt at Nineveh" (Isa. 37:37).

In this passage, the Holy Spirit, and with short shift, dispenses with Sennacherib. The word *departed* has the same meaning as a dog leaving with its tail between its legs. He went back to his capital, Nineveh.

He lived for some 18 or 20 years after this and made other military expeditions elsewhere; however, he made no further expeditions toward Jerusalem or even toward Egypt. The Jews had peace so far as the Assyrians were concerned.

In his military life, he tackled many little tin gods; however, when he faced Jerusalem, he faced the God of the ages, his creator, whether he realized it or not! It was to be an experience he would never forget!

HISTORY

"And it came to pass, as he was worshipping in the house of Nisroch his god, that Adrammelech and Sharezer his sons smote him with the sword; and they escaped into the land of Armenia: and Esar-haddon his son reigned in his stead" (Isa. 37:38).

The meaning of the phrase, *"Nisroch his god,"* refers to an eagle-headed human figure—the same as the god Asshur, the chief Assyrian deity. The corresponding goddess was Astarte.

Ancient history records that Sennacherib bequeathed his throne to his youngest son, Esar-haddon. In order to gain the favor of his god, he promised to sacrifice the two elder sons to that so-called divinity. These sons, doubtless prompted by fear on the one hand and by jealousy on the other, murdered their father in December of that year. However, six months later, they were obliged to flee to Armenia to escape the vengeance of Esar-haddon. Sennacherib's will, which bestowed the throne upon his youngest son, has recently been discovered and is now in the British museum in London.

Esar-haddon outlived Hezekiah many years and was brought into contact with Manasseh, Hezekiah's son. Sennacherib had the opportunity to accept the God of Israel, but instead, he attempted to destroy God's people. He in turn was destroyed himself.

I can see far down the mountain,
Where I've wandered many years.
Often hindered on my journey,
By the ghosts of doubts and fears.
Broken vows and disappointments,
Thickly strewn along the way.
But the Spirit has led unerring,
To the land I hold today.

HEZEKIAH

CHAPTER 6

HUMILITY

HUMILITY

"In those days was Hezekiah sick unto death. And the prophet Isaiah the son of Amoz came to him, and said unto him, Thus says the Lord, Set your house in order; for you shall die, and not live. Then he turned his face to the wall, and prayed unto the Lord, saying, I beseech You, O Lord, remember now how I have walked before You in truth and with a perfect heart, and have done that which is good in your sight. And Hezekiah wept sore. And it came to pass, afore Isaiah was gone out into the middle court, that the Word of the Lord came to him, saying, Turn again, and tell Hezekiah the captain of My people, Thus says the Lord, the God of David your father, I have heard your prayer, I have seen your tears: behold, I will heal you: on the third day you shall go up unto the house of the Lord. And I will add unto your days fifteen years; and I will deliver you and this city out of the hand of the king of Assyria; and I will defend this city for My own sake, and for My servant David's sake" (II Ki. 20:1-6).

THE PRAYER OF HEZEKIAH

How must Hezekiah have felt when Isaiah came back the second time? No doubt, when the great prophet walked through the door, one could look at his countenance and see that the message was good. What must have been Hezekiah's thoughts whenever this great message of life and living, which took the place of dying and death, was given to the king?

It's a terrible thing, I suppose, to be told that you are about to die, and that was the first message that came to the king, but now:

Oh happy day, oh happy day,
When Jesus washed my sins away,
He taught me how to watch and pray,
And keeps me singing every day,
Oh happy day, oh happy day,
When Jesus washed my sins away.

THE SALVATION OF THE SOUL

In a spiritual sense, that which happened to Hezekiah has happened to every single person who has ever been born again. The sentence of death was upon us. It was stark and cold— "You must die!" The law demanded such, and there seemed to be no way out.

But then, we heard the great story, in fact, the greatest story ever told, of Jesus and His power to save. When we said yes, the sentence of death was abated. The door to life was opened, and we were able to walk through that grand entrance—the entrance to eternal life.

When Lazarus, the friend of Christ died, the Scripture says:

Then Martha said unto Jesus, Lord, if You had been here, my brother had not died (evidently she did not seem to think of Jesus as raising her brother from the dead). *But I know, that even now, whatsoever You will ask of God, God will give it You* (the terminology used by Martha shows it was still unclear to her exactly who Jesus was). *Jesus said unto her, Your brother shall rise again* (very plainly, Jesus tells her what is about to happen; but, in her doubt, she misunderstands).

I AM THE RESURRECTION AND THE LIFE

Martha said unto Him, I know that He shall rise again in the resurrection at the last day (proclaims what she had probably learned at the feet of Jesus [Dan. 12:2, 13; Jn. 6:39-40, 44, 54; 12:48]). *Jesus said unto her, I am the resurrection, and the life* (in effect, He was saying, 'Martha, look at Me, you are looking at the resurrection and the life'; this shows that 'resurrection' and 'life' are not mere doctrines but, in reality, a person, the Lord Jesus Christ): *he who believes in Me, though he were dead, yet shall he live* (speaks of the coming resurrection of life when all the sainted dead will rise [I Thess. 4:13-18]): *And whosoever lives and believes in Me shall never die* ('whosoever believes in Me will live eternally'). *Do you believe this?* (The resurrection is the end of death; consequently, death has no more to do with the redeemed; it has done all it can do; it is finished! the redeemed live in the imparted life that put an end to it; for them, the old life, its death and judgment no longer exist) (Jn. 11:21-26) (The Expositor's Study Bible).

Now that Hezekiah had made things right with God, the Lord forgave him, added 15 years to his life, and also told him that the Assyrian effort would fail. Yet, He would deliver Jerusalem from Assyria, not because of Hezekiah or even Isaiah, but rather, He would *"defend this city for My own sake, and for My servant David's sake."*

HEALING

The Scripture says, *"Take a lump of figs. And they took and laid it on the boil, and he recovered."* This Word had evidently been given to Isaiah, and he was to give it to Hezekiah.

Why did the Lord need the figs for the healing?

The Lord didn't need the figs. In fact, the Lord needs nothing. Why He used this method, we aren't told. Really, it doesn't matter. We should be grateful for any way that He chooses to bring about healing and health to us.

Does the Lord heal presently as He did then? The Lord doesn't change. Whatever He did in Old Testament times, He did in New Testament times, and He does presently.

A PERSONAL HEALING

I can't remember exactly, but I think I was about 10 years old. For the previous six months or more during that time, I had come to the place that I was constantly nauseated. At times, I would pass out, meaning that I would literally go unconscious. In fact, this happened several times while I was at school.

The last time it happened, the principal called my parents, and they were told, "If something is not done, Jimmy is going to have to be taken out of school." Then the principal added, "We don't want him dying on our hands."

In fact, my mother and dad had taken me to several doctors, with all the ensuing examinations, and it was all to no avail. In other words, they simply did not know what was wrong with me. They ruled out malaria, plus several other things, and whatever it was they tried seemingly did not work. Instead of getting better, I was getting worse. I fully believe that Satan was trying to kill me. He knew how the Lord would use me in the future, so that was his way of stopping it. Thank the Lord, he didn't succeed.

During all of this time, I was prayed for any number of times. We had a godly pastor at our little church. He was young, but he loved the Lord and fully believed that the Lord healed the sick. Besides that, my parents, my grandmother, and my aunt strongly believed in the power of God and the ability of the Lord to heal the sick and to perform miracles, irrespective of the problem. Nevertheless, despite their anointing me with oil any number of times and repeatedly praying for me, I did not grow better, but rather worse.

THE MANNER IN WHICH
THE LORD DOES THINGS

Actually, there is no person who fully understands why the Lord does things in the manner in which they are carried out. We know that He is omnipotent, meaning all-powerful, and omniscient, meaning all-knowing, and omnipresent, meaning that He is everywhere. Consequently, He has means about which we know nothing.

On this particular day in question, actually a Sunday, my parents had invited the pastor and his wife to go with us to lunch after the service, which they did. I remember that when my parents invited Brother Culbreth, our pastor, he stated that first of all, they had to go to a particular brother's house and pray for him. It was a family that all of us knew, and who attended our little church.

That Sunday, and it must have been about 12:30 or 1 p.m., we went to the little three-room shotgun house to pray for the brother in question. I remember the pastor and his wife, my mother and dad, along with my baby sister and me, walking to the back room where the brother was. He was anointed with oil and prayer was offered for him regarding whatever type of illness he had.

We then all walked back to the front room and were standing there, in effect, making small talk with the lady of the house, planning to leave in a moment.

THE BALL OF FIRE

My dad spoke up and said to the pastor, "Brother Culbreth, please pray for Jimmy. If the Lord doesn't do something for him, we're going to have to take him out of school."

Brother Culbreth was standing there with a bottle of oil in his hand, with which he had just anointed the dear brother in question. I remember him smiling and walking across the floor to where I was standing. I can still see that room. My dad, the pastor, and his wife were standing against the back wall. My mother was to my right, along with the wife of the dear brother for whom we had just prayed. I was standing next to the door that led outside.

Brother Culbreth walked over to where I was standing, took the top off the little bottle of oil, placed a little of it on his finger, and anointed my head, with all of us beginning to pray. In fact, he had done that any number of times. However, this time, something happened, and it happened instantly.

It was like a ball of fire, something about the size of a softball, which started at the top of my head and slowly went down the back of my body, all the way to my feet, yet without any pain. Even though I was only 10 years old, and, as stated, I had been prayed for any number of times previous to this, I knew that now I was healed. There was no doubt about it; I knew I was healed.

I don't remember a great moving of the Spirit that took place in the room at that moment. I do remember everyone there praising the Lord, but again, we always did that. However, I knew I was healed.

The sickness left immediately, never came back, and I have enjoyed excellent health from then until now.

I did have a stint put in an artery of my heart in February 2001, and I've had the normal colds, and one time, I even had what is referred to as "walking pneumonia." However, relatively speaking, I've enjoyed excellent health. I've traveled all over the world and eaten food that should have made anyone sick but without any adverse affect to my physical body. I give the Lord all the praise and glory.

WHY?

Why didn't the Lord heal me when I was prayed for previously? Why did He wait until we were standing in the front room of this little house? Was it that the level of faith wasn't quite high enough as it regarded the pastor, my parents, or even me?

The answer to the question is no! The Lord is not waiting for someone's level of faith to rise to a certain level before He will do something for him. That foolishness has been taught, but it's not scripturally correct. As long as there is a flicker of faith, the Lord will honor it in one way or the other. To be sure, when people submit themselves to prayer, they're doing such because they believe. To be certain, we unequivocally believed that the Lord healed the sick, even as I still do and always will.

I don't know the answer to the first question. As to why the Lord waited this long, only He could answer that. However, one thing is certain, everything the Lord does is for purpose and reason. He does nothing according to happenstance or happenchance. Everything is by design. As well, whatever He does is done for our benefit and for our good.

PRAYER

In looking back at that scenario, I can readily tell people who have been prayed for any number of times, yet with no obvious evidence of the prayer being answered, that they should not quit. Keep believing the Lord. Keep asking. In fact, the Lord beautifully and gloriously tells us the same thing in His Word. He said:

> *Ask, and it shall be given you; seek, and you shall find; knock, and it shall be opened unto you* (all of this speaks of persistence and guarantees a positive answer, at least if it's in the will of God). *For everyone who asks receives; and he who seeks finds; and to him who knocks it shall be opened* (He says 'everyone,' and that includes you and me!). *If a son shall ask bread of any of you who is a father, will he give him a stone? or if he ask a fish, will he for a fish give him a serpent? Or if he shall ask an egg, will he offer him* (an egg containing) *a scorpion? If you then, being evil, know how to give good gifts unto your children* (means that an earthly parent certainly would not give a child a stone who has asked for bread, etc.): *how much more shall your heavenly Father give the Holy Spirit to them who ask Him?* (This refers to God's goodness and the fact that everything from the Godhead comes to us through the person and agency of the Holy Spirit; and all that He does for us is based upon the Cross of Christ and our faith in that finished work) (Lk. 11:9-13) (The Expositor's Study Bible).

THE LUMP OF FIGS

Evidently, the Lord said to the prophet Isaiah, *"Take a lump of figs."* Obviously He told the prophet to lay the lump of figs on the boil, which it seems was threatening the life of the king. The Scripture then says, *"He recovered."* Two things are said here and done. They are:

1. Why didn't the Lord heal Hezekiah exactly as He healed me and, in fact, has healed millions of others? The Lord didn't need figs, yet He told the prophet to use them.

2. As well, the word *recover* refers to the fact that Hezekiah was healed gradually.

I was healed instantly, even as millions have been healed instantly, but the king wasn't.

Why?

The Lord could have easily healed him instantly, but He chose another method. I think the only answer that can be given is according to the following: It doesn't really matter how the Lord does things, what or who He uses, or the manner or direction which it all takes. If He does it, we should be grateful and thankful in any case.

THE SUN DIAL

And Hezekiah said unto Isaiah, What shall be the sign that the Lord will heal me, and that I shall go up into the house of the Lord the third day? And Isaiah said, This sign shall you have of the Lord, that the Lord will do the thing that He has spoken:

shall the shadow go forward ten degrees, or go back ten degrees? And Hezekiah answered, It is a light thing for the shadow to go down ten degrees (forward): *no, but let the shadow return backward ten degrees. And Isaiah the prophet cried unto the Lord: and He brought the shadow ten degrees backward, by which it had gone down in the dial of Ahaz* (II Ki. 20:8-11).

The *"third day"* refers to the coming of the Messiah and that He would rise from the dead on the third day. Considering that this sign had to do with the Messiah, neither the Lord nor the prophet was angry at the request of Hezekiah. Both—going forward or backward—were impossible. However, going backward was even more impossible!

The miracle performed regarding the sundial would make a *"long day."* The event of this long day was known all over the world of that day.

With the word of its origination having spread far and wide, inquiries came from Babylon to learn more about the God who could not only stop the rotation of the earth but actually make it go backward for a period of time. Several centuries later, Greek historians informed Alexander the Great that this was one of the great wonders recorded in their scientific books.

THE SIGN

Why did Hezekiah need a sign?

Being told that death is imminent is not a very pleasant thing for one to hear. No doubt, fear, and even great fear, was in the heart of the king. To make certain of what Isaiah had told him—not that he doubted the words of the prophet—he asked for a sign.

It would be easy for us to criticize him; however, if placed in his position, quite possibly, we would have done the same thing.

At the present time, we have some 6,000 years of biblical history behind us. As well, the Cross, which opened up everything, presents a fact, and actually has been a fact for some 2,000 years. During that time frame, and due to the fact that the Holy Spirit lives permanently in the heart and life of every believer, there is far greater knowledge presently of the Lord and His Word than there was in Old Testament times. In other words, our need presently for such a sign should not be as acute as it was then.

THE CROSS

Before the Cross, the Holy Spirit was only with certain individuals, and then only for a short period of time. Now, it has totally changed in that He lives permanently within our hearts and lives (I Cor. 3:16). That makes all the difference in the world! Our access to the Lord presently is far more easily achieved than before the Cross.

That's why Paul said:

But now (since the Cross) has He (the Lord Jesus) obtained a more excellent ministry (the new covenant in Jesus' blood is superior and takes the place of the old covenant in animal blood), *by how much also He is the mediator of a better covenant* (proclaims the fact that Christ officiates between God and man according to the arrangements of the new covenant), *which was established upon better promises.* (This presents the new covenant explicitly based on the cleansing and forgiveness of all sin, which the old covenant could not do.) *For if that first covenant had been faultless* (proclaims the fact that the first covenant was definitely not faultless; as stated, it was based on animal blood, which was vastly inferior to the precious blood of Christ), *then should no place have been sought for the second* (proclaims the necessity of the new covenant) (Heb. 8:6-7) (The Expositor's Study Bible).

NO IMPOSSIBILITY WITH GOD

Hezekiah asked for a sign, and through Isaiah, the Lord told him, in essence, what the sign would be; however, he gave the king a choice. The sign concerned the sundial, and the Lord asked the king, *"Shall the shadow go forward ten degrees, or go back ten degrees?"*

Concerning the rotation of the earth, which is what the sundial represented, exactly how much Hezekiah or even Isaiah knew about all of this is anyone's guess.

For the Lord to maneuver the sundial, which involved the rotation of the earth, was a miracle in either direction. The king was wrong about one thing when he said, *"It is a light thing for the shadow to go down ten degrees."* While it was a light thing with the Lord, it was a miracle either way of astounding proportions.

So, the king asked, *"Let the shadow return backward ten degrees."* Somehow, he had it in his mind that this would be harder to do.

Either way, the Lord would either have to speed up the rotation of the earth or cause the earth to stop in its rotation and then reverse itself for a period of time, which it did.

Now some have said that the Lord simply caused the sundial to go forward but did not manipulate the earth whatsoever; however, He most definitely could have done that, but it is doubtful. Every evidence is that He literally stopped the rotation of the earth and caused it to rotate backward for the required period of time. This made for a long day. Few miracles in history, if any, have equaled this.

WHY DID THE LORD DO THIS?

Considering that this long day was known over the world of that day, this proves that the Lord did not merely manipulate the sundial. He actually caused the earth to stop in its rotation and then go backward for a period of time. The following report was given in one of the archaeological discoveries. It stated:

In the affair of the scientific inquiries, who were sent from Babel to inquire about the remarkable thing which has happened on earth, this sign and remarkable event refers to the going back of the shadow on the sundial, which was so remarkable that even the Chaldean astronomers came to inquire about the God who could turn the sun backward.

Furthermore, Greek historians informed Alexander the Great that it was one of the greatest wonders recorded in their scientific books. This shows that the happening was not merely the moving of a shadow, but rather the rotation of the earth. The matter was known in various lands, and the Chaldeans came to inquire about it when they learned it was caused by Israel's God.

THE MIRACLE

The reason that the Lord performed this notable miracle had to do with the coming of the Messiah, who, through the lineage of Hezekiah, would be born into this world. His mission was to redeem mankind, which He would do by virtue of the Cross. Consequently, this *"long day"* would be equaled out by the somewhat *"short day"* when Jesus died on Calvary (Mat. 27:45).

The *"third day"* mentioned by Hezekiah—irrespective as to what he meant by the question—represented the day that Jesus was raised from the dead, i.e., the third day.

Despite what Satan would attempt to do, and despite the unbelief of believers, so to speak, the Lord was showing that day that He had the power to get this thing done, which He did!

BABYLON

At that time Berodach-baladan, the son of Baladan, king of Babylon, sent letters and a present unto Hezekiah: for he had heard that Hezekiah had been sick. And Hezekiah hearkened unto them, and showed them all the house of his precious things, the silver, and the gold, and the spices, and the precious ointment, and all the house of his armor, and all that was found in his treasures: there was nothing in his house, nor in all his dominion, that Hezekiah showed them not. Then came Isaiah the prophet unto king Hezekiah, and said unto him, What said these men? and from whence came they unto you? And Hezekiah said, They are come from a far country, even from Babylon. And he said, What have they seen in your house? And Hezekiah answered, All the things that are in my house have they seen: there is nothing among my treasures that I have not shown them. And Isaiah said unto Hezekiah, Hear the Word of the Lord. Behold, the days come, that all that is in your house, and that which your fathers have laid up in store unto this day, shall be carried into Babylon: nothing shall be left, says the Lord. And of your sons who shall issue from you, which you shall beget, shall they take away; and they shall be eunuchs in the palace of the king of Babylon. Then said Hezekiah unto Isaiah, Good is the word of the Lord which you have spoken. And he said, Is it not good, if peace and truth be in my days? (II Ki. 20:12-19).

THE PROPHECY OF ISAIAH

Secular history relates that at this moment in history, the king of Babylon was seeking allies to strengthen him against the king of Assyria; hence, this was one of his reasons for his embassage to Hezekiah.

At this time, Babylon was not nearly the power that Nineveh was. So, the prophecy that Isaiah would shortly give concerning the coming supremacy of Babylon would certainly not seem practical at this particular time; however, as are all prophecies given by the Lord, they always come to pass exactly as stated.

Although Hezekiah's object in showing the Babylonians the house of his armor and the house of his treasures was to convince these ambassadors of the power of Judah, he would have done far better to have related to them the grace and glory of Jehovah!

THE REBUKE

As stated, Hezekiah did not show the ambassadors from Babylon the things of God, but rather the riches of Judah. He would be rebuked for it. It seems that he mentioned not at all the greatest treasure of all, the glory of God.

An old sin is an easy sin!

Verse 17 refers to the coming time when Judah would completely lose her way with God and be taken in chains to Babylon. It would be fulfilled about 125 years later.

The word *sons* in verse 18 refers to grandsons or even great-grandsons. There was no word for grandson in the Hebrew language.

The whole prophecy of verses 17 and 18 was very remarkable because Babylon was a feeble kingdom at that time.

Hezekiah accepted the rebuke, thereby, he acknowledged himself to have been in the wrong and submitted without remonstrance to his punishment. It was a relief, however, to hear that the blow would not fall during his lifetime.

WHAT HAVE THEY SEEN IN YOUR HOUSE?

As stated, an old sin is an easy sin.

The pride factor was not humbled quickly or easily. It seems that Hezekiah succumbed once more. This was even after the Lord had lengthened his days by 15 years and had given him victory over the Assyrians by a direct miracle. How hard it is for all of us to fully walk as the Lord desires that we walk.

Hezekiah answered Isaiah when the question was asked, *"What have they seen in your house?"* He said, *"All the things that are in my house have they seen."* He did not show the ambassadors from Babylon the things of God, but rather the riches of Judah. He would be rebuked for it. Actually, most of what was shown to these Babylonian emissaries, even though it would happen many years later, would be *"carried into Babylon."* The prophet said, *"Nothing shall be left, says the Lord."* This referred to the time, about 125 years later, when Judah would completely lose her way with God and be taken in chains to Babylon.

BABYLON AND NINEVEH

At the time of Hezekiah, Babylon and Nineveh were two great city-states competing for supremacy in Assyria. Actually, at this time, Babylon was not nearly the power that Nineveh was. In fact, it was far from such! So, the prophecy that Isaiah gave concerning the coming supremacy of Babylon certainly did not seem practical at this particular time. However, like all prophecies given by the Lord, they would come to pass exactly as stated.

Secular history relates that at this moment, the king of Babylon was seeking allies to strengthen Him against the king of Assyria; hence, this was one of his reasons for his embassage to Hezekiah. Quite possibly, Hezekiah agreed to help and, thereby, formed a treaty because verse 13 says, *"And Hezekiah hearkened unto them."* Hezekiah's objective in showing them the house of his armor and the house of his treasures was to convince the ambassadors of the power of Judah. As stated, he could have shown them the power of God, but instead, he did the opposite.

THE WORD OF GOD IS INFALLIBLE

"And the rest of the acts of Hezekiah, and all his might, and how he made a pool, and a conduit, and brought water into the city, are they not written in the book of the chronicles of the kings of Judah? And Hezekiah slept with his fathers: and Manasseh his son reigned in his stead" (II Ki. 20:20-21).

Actually, that conduit is still there. In fact, I saw it not long ago. Up until 2003, it was claimed by some that Hezekiah was not the one who had made this underground passage; however, archaeologists discovered proof in the latter part of 2003, which verifies the Scripture.

The truth is, the Scripture doesn't need anything to verify it; instead, all such discoveries must have the Scripture to verify them.

The Word of God is infallible, meaning it is without error, because it is the Word of God. The Bible is the only revealed truth in the world today and, in fact, ever has been.

Time is filled with swift transition,
Naught of earth unmoved can stand.
Build your hopes on things eternal,
Hold to God's unchanging hand.

Trust in Him who will not leave you,
Whatsoever years may bring,
If by earthly friends forsaken,
Still more closely to Him cling.

Covet not this world's vain riches,
That so rapidly decay,
Seek to gain the heavenly treasures,
They will never pass away.

When your journey is completed,
When the valley you pass through,
Fair and bright the home in glory,
Your enraptured soul will view.

REFERENCES

CHAPTER 1

George Williams, *William's Complete Bible Commentary*, *Grand Rapids, Kregel Publications, 1994, Pg. 339*

Ibid.

CHAPTER 2

George Williams, *William's Complete Bible Commentary*, *Grand Rapids, Kregel Publications, 1994, Pg. 254*

CHAPTER 3

George Williams, *William's Complete Bible Commentary*, *Grand Rapids, Kregel Publications, 1994, Pg. 11*

Kenneth S. Wuest, *The New Testament: An Expanded Translation, Grand Rapids, Eerdmans Publishing Company, 1961*

George Williams, *William's Complete Bible Commentary*, *Grand Rapids, Kregel Publications, 1994, Pg. 254*

ABOUT EVANGELIST JIMMY SWAGGART

The Rev. Jimmy Swaggart is a Pentecostal evangelist whose anointed preaching and teaching has drawn multitudes to the Cross of Christ since 1955.

As an author, he has written more than 50 books, commentaries, study guides, and The Expositor's Study Bible, which has sold more than 2.8 million copies.

As an award-winning musician and singer, Brother Swaggart has recorded more than 50 gospel albums and sold nearly 16 million recordings worldwide.

For more than six decades, Brother Swaggart has channeled his preaching and music ministry through multiple media venues including print, radio, television and the Internet.

In 2010, Jimmy Swaggart Ministries launched its own cable channel, SonLife Broadcasting Network, which airs 24 hours a day to a potential viewing audience of more than 1 billion people around the globe.

Brother Swaggart also pastors Family Worship Center in Baton Rouge, Louisiana, the church home and headquarters of Jimmy Swaggart Ministries.

Jimmy Swaggart Ministries materials can be found at **www.jsm.org**.

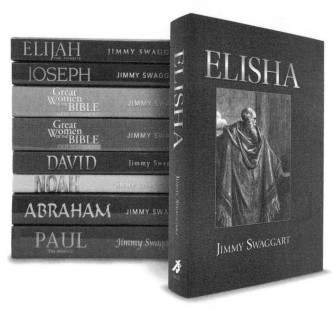